AMERICAN ART HISTORY
Volume I

by Kristin J. Draeger

ART HISTORY CURRICULUM
DISGUISED AS FUN

Contents

Introduction

Overview

This curriculum covers one semester of American art history, roughly from Pre-Columbian times to the Revolutionary War. The set consists of three parts: *American Art History: Volume I, Drawing American Art: Volume I,* and *American Art Bingo: Volume I.* The curriculum is designed to be used once a week as a supplement to any American history curriculum, and each lesson requires about two hours to complete. The lessons can be completed in any order, but I recommend the following sequence:

1.   Read a chapter in *American Art History: Volume I* and play the Forgery games.
2.   Play *American Art Bingo: Volume I.*
3.   Complete the companion drawing project in *Drawing American Art: Volume I.*

American Art History: Volume I

American Art History: Volume I is arranged chronologically and divided into sixteen chapters, each chapter introducing one or two pieces of art. One chapter should be read each week. Chapters can be read individually or aloud. Students often enjoy taking turns reading the articles aloud as a group. Teachers or parents can instigate discussions by helping to define difficult vocabulary or by asking students what is real in the article and what is added for comic effect.

The Forgery Game

Each chapter includes one to three Forgery games. The games are simple: compare the real work of art to the "forgery" on the facing page and try to find ten differences. This game can be played by students individually or in a group setting. In a group students often enjoy competing against each other to see who can find all ten differences first. The game allows children to enjoy studying art, and entices them to thoroughly examine each work of art. By spending time comparing two images, students spend time studying the art in close detail.

The Bingo Game

The *American Art Bingo Game: Volume I* provides an invaluable review, and should be played once each week. As the semester progresses the game both reviews the art students have already studied in the earlier chapters, and previews art to be studied in the future. As the teacher/parent holds up each image and calls out the name, location and date of the artwork, students inadvertently memorize the information about each piece.

The Drawing Projects

Finally, the projects in *Drawing American Art: Volume I,* allow students to kinesthetically examine each piece of art in minute detail. Provided with easy step-by-step instructions, all students can produce an impressive reproduction of one of the artworks from each chapter of *American Art History: Volume I.*

1
Prehistoric
Art

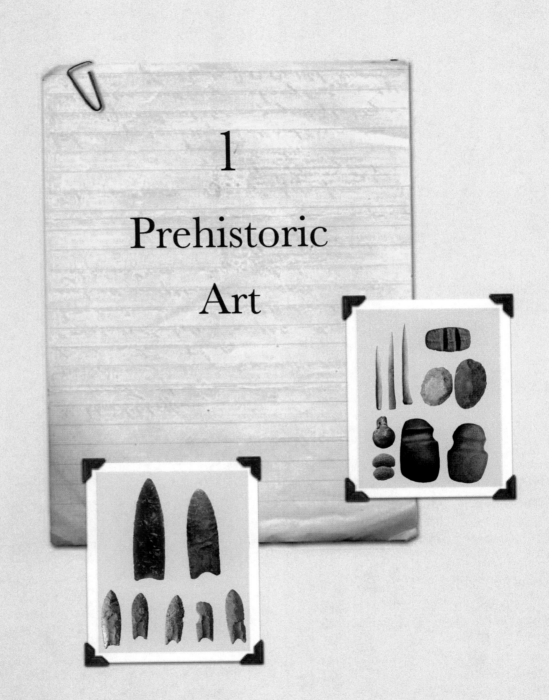

AMERICAN ART FROM THE:
CLOVIS CULTURE
North America

BEGAN
11,500 B.C.

ENDED
8000 B.C.

Clovis, New Mexico is on the Map!

CLOVIS POINTS POINT TO US

In which we learn where the term "Clovis points" came from and why it's not a good idea to leave your garbage out at night.

CLOVIS, NEW MEXICO, PRESENT DAY

This week we here at the *Prehistoric Prattle* interviewed Mr. Hiztori Izmielyfe, local amateur history buff and citizen of Clovis, New Mexico, about the famous Clovis spear points found not far from here in 1929.

"Back in 1929 this here tiny town of Clovis was just a nameless backwater burg," recounts Mr. Izmielyfe, "but in that same year fortune turned her magnificent mug toward us! It was during that year long ago that archaeologists dug up this homely little spear point, and WHAMMO! This city became famous!"

CLOVIS CULTURE

"Not only did they name the spear points Clovis points, after our humble town," continued Hiztori, "but historians also identify the group of people that produced these important artifacts as the Clovis culture," he boasted. "Of course we never met the Clovis people. Experts reckon that members of the Clovis culture trekked through North America and carved these spear points between 11,500 and 8000 B.C."

1. Clovis culture. ***Clovis Spear Points***. c. 10,000 B.C Fluted stone. Heritage of the Americas Museum, Cuyamaca College, El Cajon, California (top row). Iowa Office of the State Archaeologist Collection (bottom row).

Woolly mammoth
32 USA

Archaeologists make a point of preserving spear artifacts.

"Fortunately the site where they found the Clovis points wasn't smack dab in the middle of town or we'd be overrun by nosey archaeologists and gawking tourists. If you're interested in seeing the place it's a few miles to the south of us. They call it the Blackwater Draw Locality No. 1, after a dry stream bed that runs through the site. Leave it to the experts to make a mess of what could have been a right purty name."

"The man who discovered the Clovis points, a Mr. Ridgely Whiteman, called this here town of Clovis home," remembers Hiztori. "He had the honor of being the first to find the points, but he certainly wasn't the last to be interested. Since then dozens and dozens of them archaeologists been a swarmin' all over the site a postulatin', theorizin' and of course diggin'."

"I must admit they have found some mighty interestin' things, though, and not just spear points and tools and such, though there have been plenty of those. Apparently back in the days when them Clovis people lived here there were mammoths, camels, bison, wolves and even sabertooth cats! Imagine! Can't say I'd want to see one of them rootin' around in my garbage can after dark."

"By the way," continued Hiztori, "since that fateful day back in '29 archaeologists been findin' Clovis points all over North America, not just near the city of Clovis. Apparently back around 10,000 B.C. them points were no secret; seems everybody was using 'em."

WERE THE CLOVIS PEOPLE FIRST?
"And just because them Clovis people were the coolest culture since sliced mammoth steaks doesn't mean they were the first

group to set foot in North America. While huntin' for more Clovis crud, them experts detected signs of earlier inhabitants, though who they were and where they came from are still a mystery." At this point Mr. Izmilyfe wistfully glanced up into the sky and announced "My money is on outer space."

2. Knight, Charles R. (restorer). *Rancho La Brea Tar Pool*. 1871. Mural, 9 x 12 feet. American Museum of Natural History, New York (Photo from The Jesse Earl Hyde Collection, Case Western Reserve University Department of Geological Sciences). Two sloths *(paramylodon)* protect a fellow sloth trapped in a tar pit. Two Saber Tooth's *(Smilodon)* threaten while Mammoths wander in the distance and Condors roost above.

Forgery

Compare these artifacts with the originals on the left. Find ten differences. Answers are on page 189.

Original

Compare these artifacts with the forgeries on the right. Find ten differences. Answers are on page 189.

AMERICAN ART FROM:
PRE-COLUMBIAN AMERICA
North America

BEGAN
?

ENDED
1492 A.D.

Itchy's New Implement Emporium Opens its Doors!

In which we shamelessly give Itchy the entire edition to advertise his stuff. Good Luck, Itchy!

A NEW SUPERSTORE IN TOWN

NORTH AMERICA, PREHISTORY

Itchy's Implement Emporium, a new establishment dedicated to selling stone, bone, and pottery tools is opening its doors today in the downtown area.

"Tools are our life," comments Kant Karv, local construction worker. "They're also very time consuming to make. You either have to carve them out of bone, form them from clay, or painstakingly chip them out of solid rock. Who has time for that?" he laments.

This is the demographic that Itchy is hoping to serve. Will customers bite? Only time will tell.

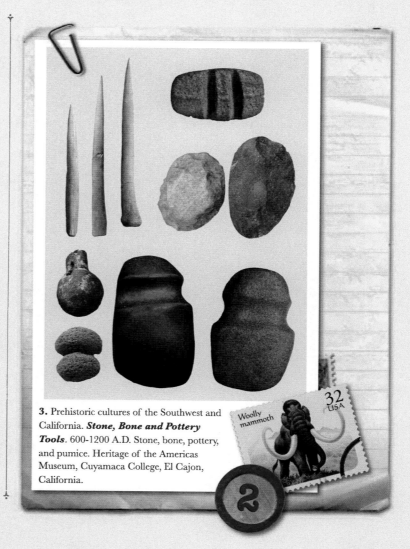

3. Prehistoric cultures of the Southwest and California. ***Stone, Bone and Pottery Tools***. 600-1200 A.D. Stone, bone, pottery, and pumice. Heritage of the Americas Museum, Cuyamaca College, El Cajon, California.

Woolly mammoth

32 USA

AT YOUR WIT'S END?

Still trying to poke a tiny needle through those thick leather hides? Poke the hole with an awl first, then watch the needle slide right through. It's awfully easy. Will modern wonders never cease?

BUY ITCHY'S AWLS FOR ALL YOUR HOLE-MAKING NEEDS!

ITCHY'S IMPLEMENT EMPORIUM

Do your arrows curve to the right or left? Do you aim for a rabbit and hit the hunter hunched next to you? An arrow shaft straightener can fix your faux-pas. Use this baby to wipe the warp out of your arrow shafts. Invest in one and you'll never return from the hunt empty-handed (or alone) again.

Come on down to

Itchy's Implement Emporium

Where stone and bone are king!

Are you a weak whistler?

Are you envious of your tooting friends?

Without the modern inventions of cell phones and email, whistling is an important skill for the average prehistoric American. But what if you just can't do it? We can help! Itchy's Implement Emporium carries all the latest in prehistoric pottery whistles. Just tie a piece of sinew to one, keep it around your neck, and you'll never need to howl like a feral fox again.

Take one home today and pucker up!

Frustrated?

Can't get all that flesh and fat off of your hides? Do your clothes smell like dead meat? Do your friends wander up wind? Use this handy hide scraper. It slices; it dices, but most importantly it smoothly scrapes excess carnage from your clothing. Come on down to Itchy' Implement Emporium and buy one today . . .

Please!

ITCHY'S IMPLEMENT EMPORIUM
Where stone and bone are king!

HERE'S A HANDY LITTLE ITEM THAT WILL CHANGE THE WAY YOU FISH FOREVER. IT'S A NET FLOAT MADE OF A REVOLUTIONARY NEW ROCK CALLED PUMICE. IT FLOATS! YES, YOU HEARD ME RIGHT. IT FLOATS IN WATER! NO MORE NETS SINKING USELESSLY TO THE BOTTOM OF THE RIVER. JUST TIE THESE BABIES TO THE TOP OF YOUR NET, TOSS IT IN AND WATCH IT FLOAT. YOU'LL NEVER HAVE TO STAND IN FRIGID WATER ALL DAY HOLDING YOUR NET AGAIN!

Come to Itchy's and buy your floats today!

Forgery

Compare these artifacts with the originals on the left. Find ten differences. Answers are on page 189.

Original

Compare these artifacts with the forgeries on the right. Find ten differences. Answers are on page 189.

2
Mound
Builder Art

MOUND BUILDER MEMO

AMERICAN ART FROM THE:
MOUND BUILDER CULTURE
Great Lakes, Ohio River Valley and
Mississippi River Valley, USA

BEGAN
c. 3400 B.C.

ENDED
c. 1500s A.D.

Birdman Tablet Wins Top Award at State Fair

In which we learn about the opposing forces of the universe and large bird schnozes.

THE BEAK SPEAKS

CAHOKIA MOUNDS, ILLINOIS, 1300 AD

Sam Sahndinnmypantz, owner of Sam's Sandstone Slabs, proudly displayed his winning sandstone tablet at the local state fair this weekend along with other tablets, clay pots and several lizard cream pies. We here at the *Mound Builder Memo* caught up with Sam later that evening and asked him to describe his monumental work.

SAM: It's a comment on the state of the cosmos. The birdman on the front (figure 4) and the serpent design on the back represent the two great opposing forces of the universe.

US: Uh, wow. We were just wondering why the man's nose is so big.

SAM: It's not a nose; it's a beak. The man in the tablet is wearing a bird mask and that rather intrusive schnoz is the beak. It matches his feathered cape and wings. It's a man in a bird costume.

US: Ah. We get it now. Then what's all that crosshatching on the back (figure 5)? Is that where you sharpen your cutting tools?

I HOPE THE WHOLE TABLET CAME IN FIRST, NOT JUST MY BEAK.

4. Mississippian Mound Builder culture. *The Birdman Tablet* (front). c. 1300 A.D. Carved sandstone, 3.6 x 2.4 inches. Illinois State Museum, Cahokia Mounds State Historic Site, Collinsville, Illinois.

5-6. Mississippian Mound Builder culture. ***The Birdman Tablet*** (back & detail). c. 1300 A.D. Carved sandstone, 3.6 x 2.4 inches. Illinois State Museum, Cahokia Mounds State Historic Site, Collinsville, Illinois.

7. *An illustration of snake skin.*

SAM: No. That is a diamond crosshatching design. It represents the scales on the skin of a serpent.

US: Okay, hmmm, then let's go back to the "state of the universe" thing. Can you tell us more about that?

SAM: Gladly. Because they fly in the sky, birds often symbolize the heavens, and the heavens represent light, order and all that's good in the universe.

The serpent, a citizen of the deep, dark, scary underground, represents darkness, chaos and everything that's wrong with the world . . . like newspapers.

US: Hey!

SAM: So a piece of art with an image of light and order on one side and darkness and chaos on the other side literally places the two forces in the universe back-to-back where they can push and pull at each other and keep the universe in balance. It's ingenious really. Brilliant. Inspired . . .

US: Like newspapers?

SAM: Um, not quite.

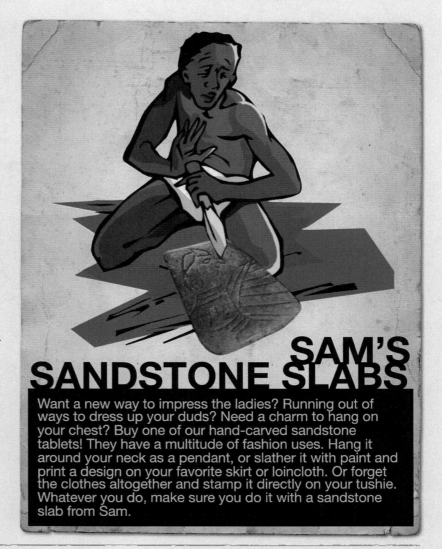

SAM'S SANDSTONE SLABS

Want a new way to impress the ladies? Running out of ways to dress your duds? Need a charm to hang on your chest? Buy one of our hand-carved sandstone tablets! They have a multitude of fashion uses. Hang it around your neck as a pendant, or slather it with paint and print a design on your favorite skirt or loincloth. Or forget the clothes altogether and stamp it directly on your tushie. Whatever you do, make sure you do it with a sandstone slab from Sam.

Forgery

Compare this artifact with the original on the left. Find ten differences. Answers are on page 189.

Original

Compare this painting with the forgery on the right. Find ten differences. Answers are on page 189.

MOUND BUILDER MEMO

AMERICAN ART FROM THE:
MOUND BUILDER CULTURE
Great Lakes, Ohio River Valley and
Mississippi River Valley, USA

BEGAN
c. 3400 B.C.

ENDED
c. 1500s A.D.

American Art History, Vol. No. 1   Bingo Card No. 4   artk12.com

It Pays to Weight!

BANNERSTONES IMPROVE THE HUNT

In which we learn about new, innovative bannerstones, and why it's good for a hunter to be in shape.

SOMEWHERE IN OHIO, 1200 AD

Having trouble with your spear thrower? Is it awkward and unbalanced? Instead of soaring weightlessly through the air does your spear crash and burn? Does your prey snicker when they see you coming?

If these things happen to you, then you will be delighted with the newest invention to come out of the Mound Association for the Improvement of Missiles (MAIM). They have recently released their Spear Thrower 2.0, a technological advancement of mind-blowing proportions.

HELP FOR YOUR BALANCE

The revolutionary innovation of the Spear Thrower 2.0 is its bannerstone. A bannerstone is a carved weight that sits on the end of the spear thrower and helps balance it so that catapulting the spear is a breeze.

A HUNTER SPEAKS

"I never knew that launching a spear could be so effortless," testifies Klumsi Klodd, local hunter and spear aficionado. The last time I went hunting I only nicked my prey on the hiney and it chased me for 6 miles! This new version of the Spear Thrower is going to change my life."

8. Hopewell and Temple II Mound Builder cultures. ***Mound Builder Bannerstones***. c. 300-1200 A.D. Carved stone. Heritage of the Americas Museum, Cuyamaca College, El Cajon, California.

A Sleek Technique
WHO MAKES THESE THINGS ANYWAY?

SOMEWHERE IN OHIO, 1200 AD

"Well, in this neck of the woods, it's me." states Stil Grindinn, bannerstone creator extraordinaire. "But who started the trend ages ago? No idea. What I can tell you is that making bannerstones is a difficult and time-consuming process."

CHOOSE A PATTERN

"First I choose a pattern. I design bannerstones in a variety of shapes and sizes, but there is a wee bit of science involved. The overall shape of the bannerstone is important; it has to be aerodynamic. A bannerstone not only weights the spear thrower, it also directs the air flow around it so that when a hunter launches his spear, the movement is completely silent. It helps when sneaking up on massive and potentially peeved animals," Stil explains.

PICK A ROCK

"After I've decided on a pattern I pick out a suitable rock; I use a variety of stones with different patterns, colors and textures.

GET IN SHAPE

Then I use a harder rock to shape it. This is the long, tedious part that requires a lot of grinding and rubbing. We have no iron or steel saws to make the process faster. In fact, I don't even know what iron and steel are!"

THE NEW
THE REVOLUTIONARY

SPEAR THROWER 2.0
BROUGHT TO YOU BY MAIM • LOCAL CHAPTER

HI, MY NAME IS STEVE,

and I like to eat meat just like the next guy, but I wouldn't be eating meat at all if it weren't for MAIM's new Spear Thrower 2.0. With the Spear Thrower 2.0 I can nail my prey at 50 yards without major injury to myself or my hunting buddies. That's right. From fifty yards as silently as a bug smacking the windshield (whatever that is). So stop scrounging for roots and grubs and go out and buy yourself a Spear Thrower 2.0. You'll never regret it. I know I won't!

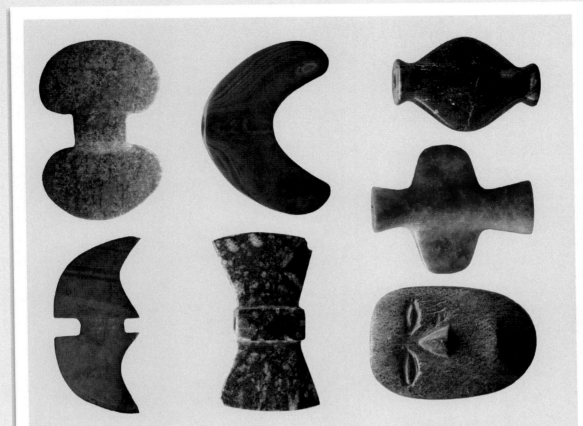

Forgery

Compare these artifacts with the originals on the left. Find ten differences. Answers are on page 189.

Original

Compare these artifacts with the forgeries on the right. Find ten differences. Answers are on page 189.

3
Native
Southwest
Art

SOUTHWEST SCANDAL

American Art History, Vol. No. 1   Bingo Card No. 5   artk12.com

AMERICAN ART FROM THE:
MIMBRES CULTURE
New Mexico, US

BEGAN
1000 A.D.

ENDED
1130 A.D.

A Death Blow on a Death Bowl

In which we learn how the Mimbres bury their dead and why it's good to be a fast runner.

OBITUARIES

MIMBRES RIVER VALLEY, NEW MEXICO, CA. 1100 AD

We who live here in the Mimbres River Valley are proud to be part of the Mimbres culture. Our culture is part of a larger group called the Mogollon culture. Mogollon people have flourished here in the Desert Southwest since about 150 AD and probably will until 1450 AD (just a hunch).

Today we here at the *Southwest Scandal* are grieved to report that one of our small group has passed on. Eyedident Runfasstinuf, legendary mountain lion hunter, died on the job this week at the ripe old age of 37.

Mr. Runfasstinuf will be buried tomorrow near the Mimbres River in the traditional manner. His body will be placed in a pit under the floor of his home in a sitting position with his knees and hands tucked under his chin (figure 9). Some of his personal belongings will be added to the pit and then the ceremony will begin.

THE CEREMONY

The ceremony is simple. As we villagers pay our respects, the village shaman will hold a

9. Draeger, Kristin after J. Walter Fewkes. ***Mimbres Burial Pit***. 2012. Drawing.

Mimbres bowl USA37

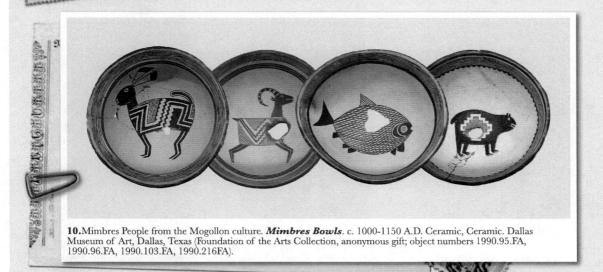

10. Mimbres People from the Mogollon culture. ***Mimbres Bowls***. c. 1000-1150 A.D. Ceramic, Ceramic. Dallas Museum of Art, Dallas, Texas (Foundation of the Arts Collection, anonymous gift; object numbers 1990.95.FA, 1990.96.FA, 1990.103.FA, 1990.216FA).

ceramic bowl (figure 10) with an image of an animal or person artfully painted in the center, then, after performing the appropriate rites, the shaman will pierce the image on the bowl with a sharpened stone. The resulting hole is called a "kill hole." He will then reverently place the bowl upside-down upon Eyedident's head.

A METAPHOR

This bowl represents the dome of the heavens above our heads. And the hole in the bowl represents the "hole" in the sky through which Eyedident's spirit will break out of the universe and enter its eternal dwelling place.

Rest in peace, Eyedident.

Mr. Runfasstinuf is survived by a wife, four children and a pet roadrunner named Bill.

WANTED
Expert Potter

Do you enjoy playing in the mud? Like to get your hands dirty? Have a hankering to create cool crocks?

If you have the following qualifications come to Pete's Pottery Pen in the Mimbres River Valley.

All applicants must be able to roll a lump of clay into a long even rod, coil into the shape of a bowl or jar, and smooth it to perfection.

Must be able to grind *kaolin* (a kind of white clay) into a fine powder and make it into smooth white *slip* (watery clay) for covering the pottery.

Applicants must then be able to burnish the dried slip to a smooth sheen. Must be skilled in grinding mineral pigments, and painting exquisite geometric, animal and human designs.

Finally you must be able to build a roaring hot fire for the kilns. Please bring tools and references.

Ability to make your own brushes and a tasty lizard stew a plus!

PETE'S POTTERY PEN

THE BEST!

IS YOUR COOKWARE GOING TO POT?

Can't contain your contempt for your shabby worn out crocks? Do your eyes glaze over when you think of replacing them? Give your old bowls the slip and come on down to Pete's Pottery Pen. Located in the beautiful Mimbres River Valley in Southwestern New Mexico, Pete's Pottery Pen offers a tremendous selection of dishes, cups, plates and other cookware. You'll be bowled over by Pete's commitment to quality, and jarred by his low, low prices.

You'll Never Shop Anywhere Else!

COME TO THE

MIMBRES RIVER VALLEY

VACATION IN SUNNY, SOUTHERN NEW MEXICO

Fed by runoff from frigid winter snows in the Black Mountains, the Mimbres River, or "River of the Willows," seasonally waters the desert landscape of the beautiful Mimbres River Valley. Located in the northern reaches of the Chihuahuan Desert, the Mimbres River Valley offers fun, sun, and a variety of desert flora and fauna, including the famous ocotillo plant (pictured above), for the visitor to enjoy. Come relax in one of our quaint pueblos and shop from one of our local pottery vendors. But don't wait. Our culture is outstanding, but it won't last long. By 1130 A.D. we are scheduled to mysteriously die out. So come linger in our locale today before we disappear forever!

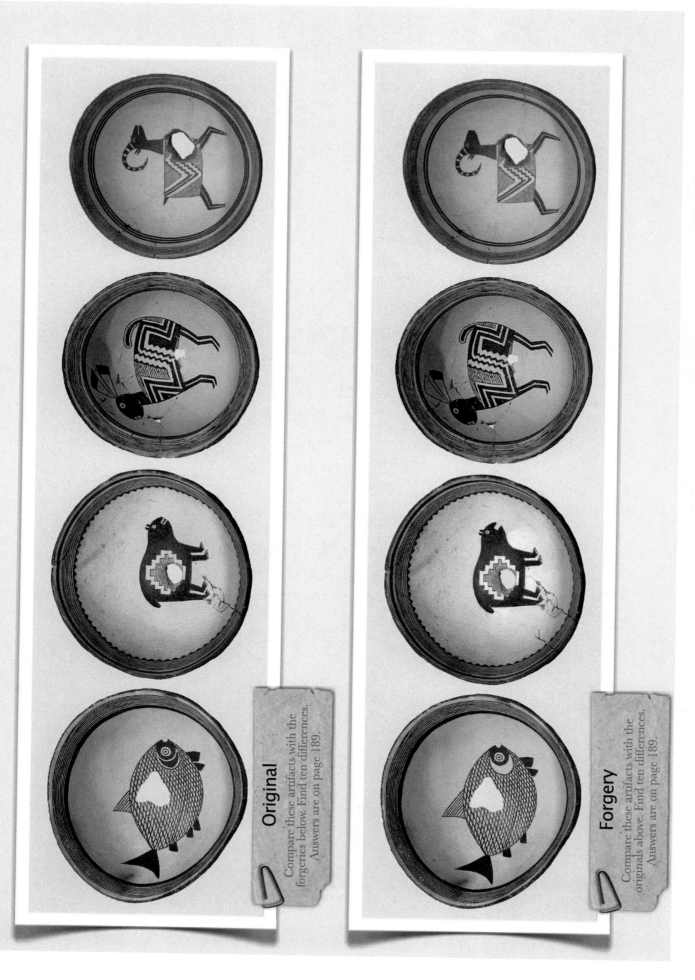

Original

Compare these artifacts with the
forgeries below. Find ten differences.
Answers are on page 189.

Forgery

Compare these artifacts with the
originals above. Find ten differences.
Answers are on page 189.

SOUTHWEST SCANDAL

AMERICAN ART FROM THE:
ANASAZI CULTURE
UT, CO, AZ, NM, USA

BEGAN
C. 1 AD

ENDED
C. 1300 AD

If the Sandal Fits, Wear It

In which we learn all we ever wanted to know about making yucca sandals, and then some.

BECAUSE THE SAND IS LAVA-HOT OUT THERE

SOMEWHERE IN THE FOUR CORNERS AREA, 1300 AD

Today we here at the *Southwest Scandal* are visiting a Mr. Weevmi Uhloan, one of the most celebrated sandal makers in all of the Anasazi territory (the pink territory on the map). He has agreed to explain to us the process of how the Anasazi, or Ancient Puebloans, make sandals here in the Desert Southwest.

SCANDAL: I guess the first obvious question would be about materials. It's really hot and dry here so there aren't many animals to provide leather, and plastic hasn't been invented yet, so what do you make your sandals out of?

UHLOAN: Good question. We make our sandals from the same material that we make almost everything else out of: yucca.

SCANDAL: Sounds yucky. What is it?

UHLOAN: It's a spiky green plant that grows rampant here it in the desert. The yucca plant loves "hot and dry" like a dog likes "dead and smelly."

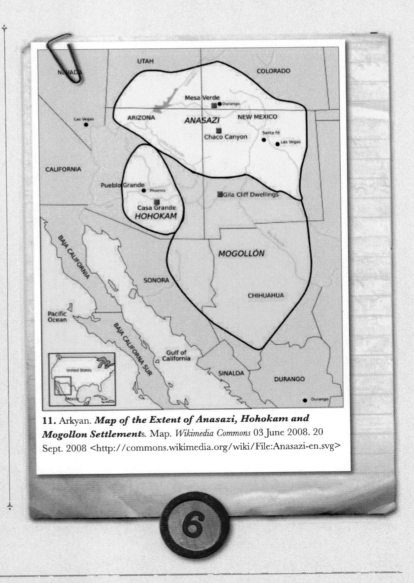

11. Arkyan. *Map of the Extent of Anasazi, Hohokam and Mogollon Settlement*s. Map. *Wikimedia Commons* 03 June 2008. 20 Sept. 2008 <http://commons.wikimedia.org/wiki/File:Anasazi-en.svg>

6

12-13. Ancient Puebloan Cultures. *Anasazi Sandal*. 400-1200 A.D. Woven Yucca Fibers. Heritage of the Americas Museum, Cuyamaca College, El Cajon, California.
14. Ancient Puebloan Culture. *Anasazi Sandal*. 700 - 1100 AD. Woven Yucca Fiber. Museum Collections of Zion National Park.
15. Chaco Anasazi Culture. *Anasazi Sandal*. 1100-1200 AD. Woven Yucca Fiber. L 26.2 cm, W 11.3 cm, T 1.7 cm. Chaco Culture National Historic Park.

SCANDAL: Lovely. What does it look like?

UHLOAN: It grows pretty low to the ground and has dozens of long, narrow, pointy leaves. The leaves are kind of thick and fleshy; they look and feel like the leaves on the top of a pineapple, but they are much bigger.

SCANDAL: How do you make sandals out of them? You can't just pull the leaves off and wrap them around your feet, they're too green and juicy.

UHLOAN: No, you can't. But it's not thefleshy part that we use, it's the long fibers inside the leaves that make good weaving material.

SCANDAL: How do you get to those fibers?

UHLOAN: First you have to break the leaves down.

SCANDAL: How do you do that; whack them with a stick?

UHLOAN: You could. Different tribes process them using different methods. Some crush the leaves and then scrape the flesh off the fibers. Others boil or roast the leaves to soften the flesh. Then they chew them clean.

SCANDAL: Chew them?

UHLOAN: Yep. Chewing helps loosen the fibers and remove the flesh. It also keeps your teeth well-flossed. All dentists in the area recommend it.

SCANDAL: I see. Are there any other methods?

UHLOAN: Sure, you can also pound, shred, or freeze them. Anything that damages them works; the more violent the better. Processing yucca leaves can be a great stress reliever.

SCANDAL: Okay, so after you've released your pent up anger and loosened up the fibers what's next?

UHLOAN: Next we spin the fibers into strands, kind of like people in other cultures spin wool or cotton. Then we twist two or three strands together to make cords or yarn.

SCANDAL: Wow, all that just to get yarn?

UHLOAN: Yep, making sandals is not for the faint of heart, or the lazy.

SCANDAL: Does all yucca yarn look the same?

UHLOAN: Not at all. Some is thin and fine; some is thick and coarse. It just depends on how much time is taken in the processing. Notice the difference in the yarns used in the sandals above (figures 12-15).

SCANDAL: I see. Okay, so we have processed our fibers into yarn. Now what?

UHLOAN: Now we weave.

SCANDAL: Weave? We just got here!

UHLOAN: Not leave. Weave. We weave the yucca yarn into sandals.

SCANDAL: Ah. How?

UHLOAN: Well, there are three basic weaving patterns. There is what is called the "plain weave," this is the easiest and most common. Figures 12, 13 and 14 are all plain weave sandals. In fact over half of our sandals are plain weave sandals.

Chewing helps loosen the fibers and remove the flesh.

IT ALSO KEEPS YOUR TEETH WELL-FLOSSED.

SCANDAL: If all three sandals are woven with the same pattern, why do they look so different?

UHLOAN: It's because they are woven with different qualities of fibers. The leaves in figure 12 have barely been processed at all; the fibers in figure 14 have been roughly processed and the fibers in figure 13 have been very finely processed, but the weaving pattern is the same in all three.

SCANDAL: Got it. What's the next weaving pattern?

UHLOAN: The second method is called "twining." With this method you have to twist and turn the yarn while you weave. Sorry, I don't have a sample sandal for this type of construction.

SCANDAL: No problem.

UHLOAN: The last is called "plaiting" which is basically like braiding hair; "plaiting" is just a fancy name for it. The sandal in figure 15 is woven using the plaiting method of construction.

SCANDAL: Do you ever get the urge to decorate your sandals?

UHLOAN: Sure. Sometimes we embroider designs on the sandals or dye the yarn. We have a variety of vegetable and mineral colors to choose from: red, yellow, black, white and even blue and green.

SCANDAL: Cool. Do you ever make anything else from yucca other than sandals?

UHLOAN: Of course. We make blankets, baskets, quivers, mats, bags, leggings, socks, belts, aprons, kilts, and even a few shirts.

SCANDAL: I bet the socks are pretty scratchy.

UHLOAN: You get used to it.

SCANDAL: What about styles? Obviously not all the sandals are the same.

UHLOAN: We have as many styles of sandals as we have species of lizards, and trust me, that's a lot. Our sandals come in a variety of toe and heel styles with many different types of ties. The toes can be square, round, or pointed. The heels can also be square, round, pointed or drawn up into a cup shape like the sandal in figure 13. So you can see that there are many possibilities.

SCANDAL: Sweet. Well, thanks for your time, Mr. Uhloan, it's been very interesting.

UHLOAN: Weaving so soon?

SCANDAL: Ha ha. Yep. I've got another appointment at noon to interview a lizard chef. Should be interesting.

UHLOAN: Lizards can cook?

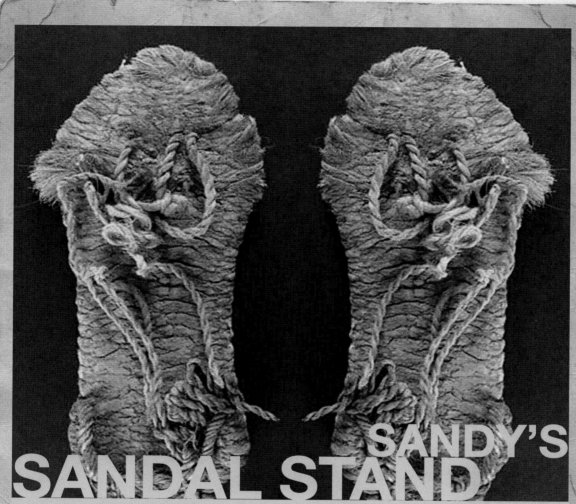

SANDY'S SANDAL STAND

Tired of toasting your tender tootsies on the hot desert sand? Been stung by a scorpion just one too many times? Stink bugs sticking between your toes? Can't stand the sand? Come on down to Sandy's Sandal Stand. At Sandy's Sandal Stand we use only the finest yucca yarn produced from Grade-A yucca leaves. Our team of skilled weavers produces sandals unmatched in quality. Each sandal is hand woven in a variety of shapes and patterns to fit your distinctive lifestyle. So try on one of our sandals and you'll find out why Sandy's Sandal Stand stands above the rest in quality, style, and comfort. Remember, it's Sandy's Sandal Stand. We don't just make sandals, we put our soles into them.

Original

Compare these artifacts with the
forgeries below. Find ten differences.
Answers are on page 189.

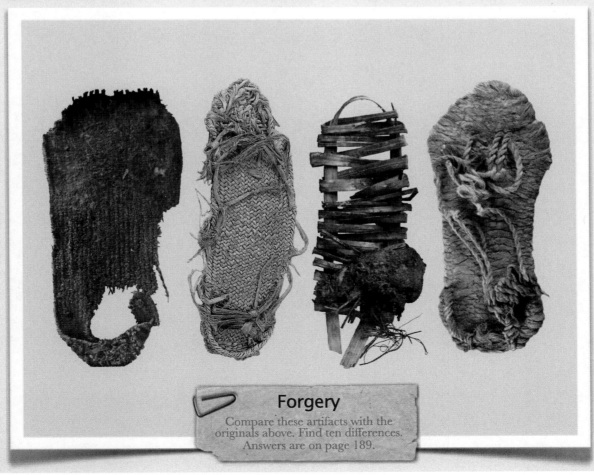

Forgery

Compare these artifacts with the
originals above. Find ten differences.
Answers are on page 189.

4
Iroquois
Art

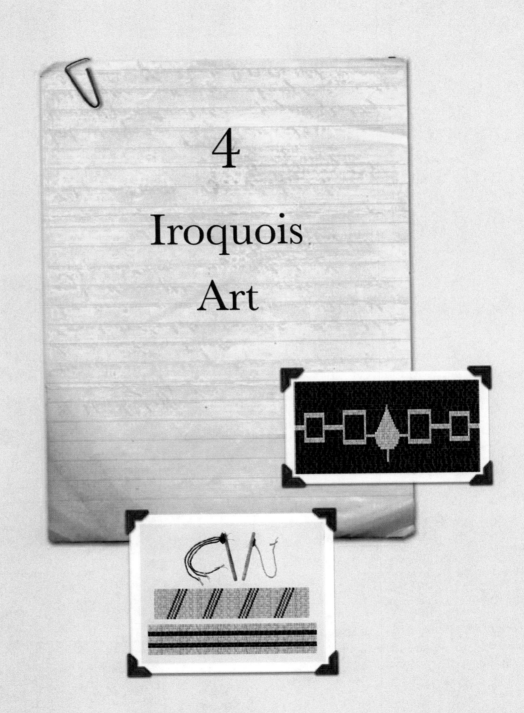

AMERICAN ART FROM THE:
IROQUOIS CULTURE
New York area, US

BEGAN c. 1000 B.C. | **CONTINUES** to present

In which we discuss the Iroquois Confederacy, the Great Tree of Peace and why wampum briefs are a bad idea.

Burying the Hatchet under the Great Tree of Peace

OR WHY CINDERELLA NEVER WORE SHELL SLIPPERS

SOMEWHERE IN THE NEW YORK AREA, PRESENT DAY

Yesterday, Mr. Ahlkeepyu Institchez, of the Iroquois Document Society, brought the old *Hiawatha Wampum Belt* to our office where we interviewed him to get an understanding of the belt and its place in Iroquois history.

QUIBBLER: Our first question may be rather obvious, but who is Hiawatha?

INSTITCHEZ: He is the legendary founder of the Iroquois Confederacy. He followed the Great Peacemaker and helped begin to bring together some of the Iroquois tribes into what eventually became the Iroquois Confederacy.

QUIBBLER: When did this happen?

INSTITCHEZ: Historians are not sure. Experts place the life of Hiawatha and the Great Peacemaker anywhere from 1142 to sometime in the 1500s A.D.

QUIBBLER: When was the Hiawatha Wampum Belt made?

16. Iroquois Culture. ***Hiawatha Wampum Belt***. Original made of shell and sinew. This is a computer graphic replica of the original held at the Library of Congress.

WOW! WHO WOULD HAVE GUESSED THAT I COULD INSPIRE SUCH A BEAUTIFUL PIECE OF ART!

INSTITCHEZ: That's hard to say too. This belt is a reproduction of the real Hiawatha belt. The real belt is in pretty bad shape.

And what we call the real Hiawatha belt is likely not the original belt that is described in the Iroquois Constitution, but is probably a reproduction from the mid 1700s.

QUIBBLER: How do you know?

INSTITCHEZ: Good question. Look at the real belt, the old one. Now look at that bead right there, in the middle, the one that looks a little different. You can see it in person; unfortunately it doesn't show up in the photograph.

QUIBBLER: You mean that one?

INSTITCHEZ: No, thats a crumb from the acorn butter sandwich that I had at lunch.

QUIBBLER: Oh, you mean that one.

INSTITCHEZ: Yes. It's different than the other beads; it's made of glass.

QUIBBLER: So?

INSTITCHEZ: Well, all the rest of the beads are made from shells. The Iroquois didn't use glass. This means that it must have been made after the colonists arrived and started making glass.

QUIBBLER: I see. I've never seen shells lying on the beach that look like these beads. Where did they find these?

INSTITCHEZ: They didn't find them in bead form; they carved them. It's a long arduous process that requires a lot of rubbing and sanding and hole-drilling, all done with rocks.

QUIBBLER: How did they make that great purple color; did they paint it?

INSTITCHEZ: No. The purple shells come from Quahog shells (figure 18), otherwise known as clams, and the creamy white ones come from the Channeled Whelk

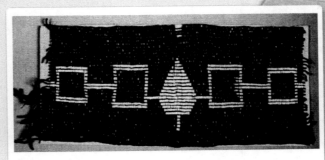

17. Iroquois Culture. ***Hiawatha Wampum Belt***. 1600s A.D. Woven shell and sinew. Library of Congress, Washington, D.C.

shell (figure 19).

QUIBBLER: Okay, and now for the big question, why a wampum belt? Why not a wampum scarf, wampum shoes, or a pair of wampum briefs?

INSTITCHEZ: Well, traditionally we Iroquois didn't write things with pen and paper like some cultures. Instead, we made belts to symbolize treaties, alliances or historical events. Besides, wampum briefs would be just too darn uncomfortable.

QUIBBLER: Good point. Okay, why did they choose purple and white shells? Why not orange and mauve or pink and chartreuse?

INSTITCHEZ: First of all it's hard to find a chartreuse shell, but besides that, the colors are symbolic: purple represents the sky, and white symbolizes purity.

QUIBBLER: Interesting. What are the squares and that "leaf-thingy" in the middle?

INSTITCHEZ: The squares represent the four Iroquois tribes in the same order that they appear on the map (figure 20).

"I am Dekanawidah [the Great Peacemaker] and…I plant the Tree of Great Peace…there beneath the shade of the spreading branches of the Tree of Peace … shall you sit and watch the Council Fire of the Confederacy of the Five Nations…"

-The Constitution of the Iroquois Nations.

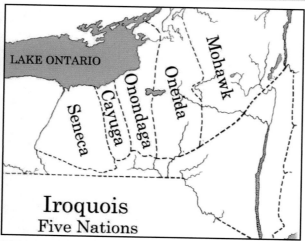

LAKE ONTARIO

Mohawk

Oneida

Onondaga

Cayuga

Seneca

Iroquois
Five Nations

18. NOAA Photo Library.
*Northern Quahog
Shell*. Photograph.

19. ChildofMidnight.
Large Eastern Conch.
Photograph.

20. R. A. Nonenmacher.
*Iroquois Five-Nations
Map c. 1650*. Map.

The 'leaf-thingy' in the middle is the Great Tree of Peace under which the hatchets were buried. It represents the Onondaga tribe. The Onondaga tribe is the capital of the Iroquois Confederacy. If you look at the map you'll see that it is in the middle of the five tribes just like the "leaf thingy" is in the middle the four squares on the belt.

QUIBBLER: I see. You mentioned they buried hatchets. Does that mean that if I go find this so-called "Tree of Peace" and dig underneath it I'll find some old decomposing hatchets? Those could be worth something, you know.

INSTITCHEZ: Uh, don't get too excited. The hatchets are just metaphorical or symbolic. "Burying the hatchet" means ending the fighting or becoming peaceful.

QUIBBLER: I get it. No more hacking each other up like tomorrow's firewood.

INSTITCHEZ: Something like that.

QUIBBLER: And I see that all the squares are connected. What does that mean?

INSTITCHEZ: It represents an alliance; the five tribes are allies. We're friends, connected by a treaty.

QUIBBLER: But why do the paths trail off the edge? Are there a lot of cliffs in your neck of the woods?

INSTITCHEZ: Um, no. The trail of white beads that runs off each side symbolizes an invitation. Anyone who is willing to "bury the hatchet" may join the confederacy. Our door is always open.

QUIBBLER: Must be cold in the winter.

INSTITCHEZ: Um, yeah.

QUIBBLER: By the way, why are the Iroquois called Iroquois?

INSTITCHEZ: Actually, that is a name given to them by French fur traders. The Iroquois call themselves Haudenosaunee.

QUIBBLER: Haudenosaunee? What does it mean?

INSTITCHEZ: Translated, it means "people of the longhouse."

QUIBBLER: What's a longhouse?

INSTITCHEZ: It's the type of building the Iroquois originally lived in.

QUIBBLER: I see. Last question. Why didn't Cinderella wear shell slippers?

INSTITCHEZ: Because shellfish and pumpkins are mortal enemies; everyone knows that.

QUIBBLER: ?

THAT SURE WAS A STRANGE ENDING, TOTO.

WOOF!

Need to see some shells? Come to

Wally's Wampum World

By the string or by the pound

Wally's Wampum is the best deal around!

Need to make a belt to record an important treaty?

Want to stitch together a new alliance?

Have a hankering to immortalize an important event? Wander over to Wally's Wampum World. Our beads are made from the highest quality shells. Our purple beads are hand-shaped from the finest Quahog shells and our creamy white beads are formed from Grade-A Channeled Whelk shells. Our artisans hand grind each bead into a tube shape, uniform in width and length, then grind a hole down the center and painstakingly polish them to perfection!

For the best beads in town, come see Wally TODAY!

Original

Compare this artifact with the forgery
below. Find ten differences.
Answers are on page 189.

Forgery

Compare this artifact with the original
above. Find ten differences.
Answers are on page 189.

AMERICAN ART FROM THE:
IROQUOIS CULTURE
New York area, USA

BEGAN c. 1000 AD | CONTINUES to present

Reading Between the Lines

In which we learn what some purple lines mean and why dependence isn't always a bad thing.

MORE WAMPUM BELTS AND STRINGS

SOMEWHERE IN THE NEW YORK AREA, PRESENT DAY

Since he did such a good job explaining the *Hiawatha Wampum Belt*, we decided to return to Mr. Ahlkeepyu Institchez of the Iroquois Document Society, for enlightenment on three other pieces of Iroquois art: the *Coming of the White Face*s wampum belt, and the *Two Row* wampum treaty.

QUIBBLER: Let's start with the *Coming of the White Faces* wampum belt. Could you explain the significance?

INSTITCHEZ: My pleasure. Adjusting to life on a new continent proved difficult for the Europeans. In fact they relied upon our help on so many occasions that our wampum keepers commissioned this wampum belt to commemorate their dependence.

QUIBBLER: Commemorating their *dependence*? I've never heard of that.

INSTITCHEZ: Don't take it wrong. It's not a bad thing. They just wanted to remember the time when their help was needed and appreciated.

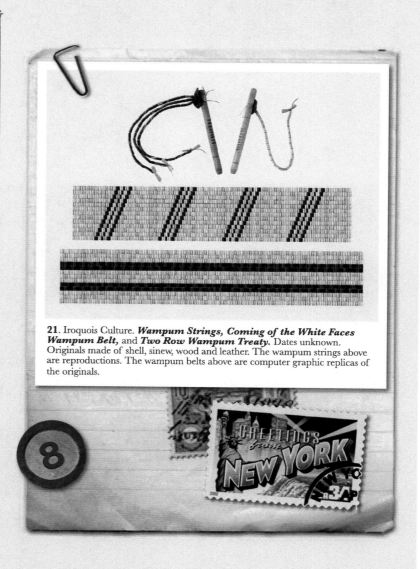

21. Iroquois Culture. ***Wampum Strings, Coming of the White Faces Wampum Belt,*** and ***Two Row Wampum Treaty.*** Dates unknown. Originals made of shell, sinew, wood and leather. The wampum strings above are reproductions. The wampum belts above are computer graphic replicas of the originals.

The purple lines symbolize the paths of two canoes crossing a river of white.

WE'LL FOLLOW OUR PATH AND YOU FOLLOW YOURS.

QUIBBLER: Got it. So how does this belt do that?

INSTITCHEZ: The belt's design contains three purple lines running diagonally across a background of white wampum. The thin purple diagonal line in the middle of each set represents you, the "white faces," the Europeans. And the thicker purple lines on the outside of each thin line represent us, the Iroquois.

QUIBBLER: So you guys were thick and strong when we were thin and weak.

INSTITCHEZ: Exactly. And the thick strong lines are supporting the thin weak line just like we supported the newcomers.

QUIBBLER: Cool. What about the other one, the *Two Row* wampum treaty. What's that all about?

INSTITCHEZ: The two purple lines symbolize the paths of two canoes crossing a river of white. One path represents the culture of the Iroquois and one path represents the culture of the Europeans.

Essentially the two groups made a deal. The Iroquois would follow their path, keeping their customs and upholding their laws and the colonists would do the same. The two cultures would peacefully lead separate lives, and peacefully follow separate paths. Both parties were hopeful that the treaty would keep the peace forever.

QUIBBLER: Well, that boat sprang a leak pretty quickly.

INSTITCHEZ: In a manner of speaking, yes. The two groups sporadically warred with each other and eventually the colonists dominated the land.

Today the belt symbolizes a lost hope, but we keep it around to remind ourselves of what we lost and what might have been.

Walter's Wampum Strings

Thinking about sending a message?

Need to call a council meeting?
Announce a birth?
Elect a chief?

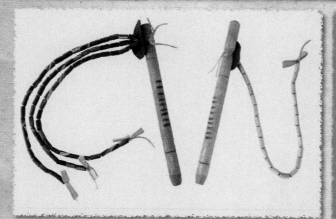

Can't depend upon your teenage son's gnat-sized attention span to deliver your message intact? Send him on his errand carrying one of Walter's Wampum strings! Walter's Wampum Strings convey the correct message, every time.

Check out some of Walter's finest work in the photo above.

Three purple strings of wampum means a chief has died and the people are called to a meeting to mourn him.

One white string calls everyone to a religious council.

Walter's Wampum Strings match the color and the pattern to the content correctly. They won't signal a birth when you are mourning a death, and they won't call an election when you just want to tell Uncle Truman that you caught a possum for dinner.

Walter's Wampum Strings are crafted from top-notch materials. And speaking of notches, Walter never gets the notches wrong. The number of notches on the stick will tell how many days until the event. Period.

Remember, for quality and accuracy it's Walter's Wampum Strings.

Always right. *Every time*.

Council Meeting Tonight

Twice every year we Iroquois hold a council meeting to review our history and tonight is the night! At 7:00 at the longhouse of Mr. Myhausiz Jyenormuss, the current Wampum Keepers will pass around each belt and string in their care and recount their stories. Remember, we do this not to put small children to sleep, but to ensure that our important documents and records are not forgotten.

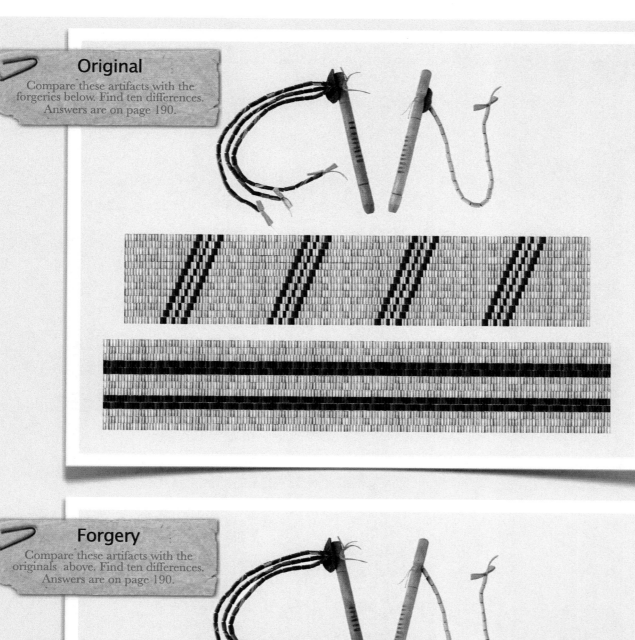

Original

Compare these artifacts with the forgeries below. Find ten differences. Answers are on page 190.

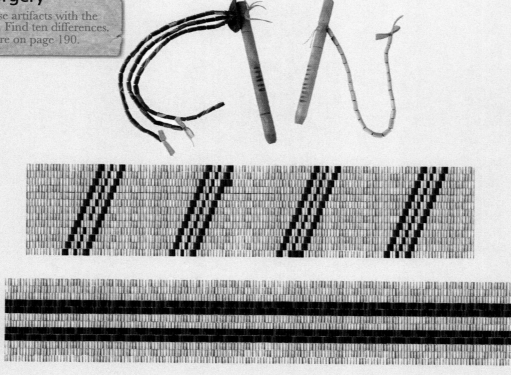

Forgery

Compare these artifacts with the originals above. Find ten differences. Answers are on page 190.

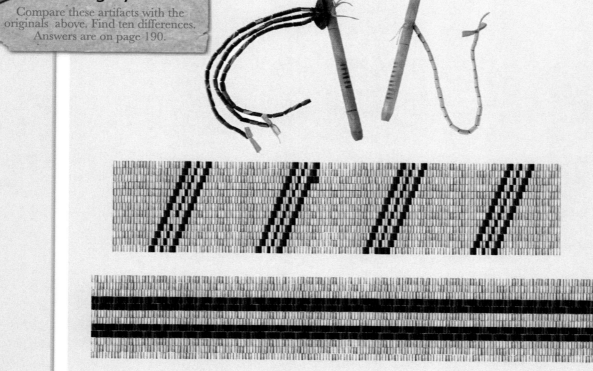

5
Taino
Art

TAINO TATTLER

ART FROM THE:
TAINO CULTURE
Bahamas, Greater Antilles, Lesser Antilles

BEGAN c. 600 A.D.

CONTINUES to present

American Art History, Vol. No. 1   Bingo Card No. 9   artk12.com

Dead Son Makes Miracle

In which we read some very old myths about bones turning into fish.

TURNS OWN BONES INTO FISH

HISPAÑOLA, IN MYTHIC TIME

Once upon a time, Yaya and his wife (the oldest resident gods of our venerable island of Hispañola), received a surprise gift from their dead (yes, dead) son, Yayael.

"It's not everyday your dead relatives send you gifts." commented Yaya. "It sort of took us by surprise, to say the least."

"This is how it happened. My wife and I were out digging roots in the cassava fields around noon. The sun was beating down on us something fierce and all of a sudden I got a hankering to see the bones of our son. Of course, in the ancient Taino tradition our son's remains rest peacefully in a hollowed out gourd hanging from the rafters of our home." he explained.

"So Ma and I hefted our digging tools onto our shoulders and walked back to the house. Ma carefully climbed up onto the table (I've got a bad back) and unhooked the gourd."

"Lowering it gingerly with both hands, she

22. Taino Culture. ***Zemi of Deminan Caracaracol***. c. 1200-1492 A.D. Originals made of clay. This statue is a reproduction. Original is part of the collection of the National Museum of the American Indian, Washington, D.C.

WE'RE GOING TO TURN INTO WHAT?

23. Theodor de Bry(1528-1598) after John White. ***Natives Barbecuing Fish.*** Engraving. 1590.

angled it toward me and I peered inside. And I'll be a lizard on a horse fly farm if those dried up old bones weren't gone! Instead, I saw live fish flopping and a swimming in the bottom of the gourd!"

"Well, we stood there dumbstruck like," continued Yaya, "trying to make heads or tails of the situation, when Ma here took control. She caught those scaly critters one by one, took them outside and barbecued them."

"Soon I smelled the warm sweet smell of a new kind of meat cooking on the barbie. When they finished cooking, I have to say I was a might jumpy about eating anything that was once a member of our family. But I pinched off a bit of the flaky white stuff and chawed it."

"Well I'll be a cold iguana on a hot day if that fish wasn't just as tasty as grubs in pineapple sauce! If it wasn't for our son it would never have occurred to us to eat fish. Imagine."

"Now," concluded Yaya, "I'm fixing to build a contraption to catch more of them out in the ocean. And from now on every time we eat fish, we'll think of Yayael and thank him for his tasty gift."

Quadruplets Raid Yaya's Home

CAUSE FLOODING WORLDWIDE

HISPANOLA, IN MYTHIC TIME

Police apprehended a set of eighteen-year-old, male quadruplets today for illegal home entry and attempted burglary.

"They ransacked the house and plundered the contents of Yaya's magic gourd," reported Katchin Badgyes, detective for the local police force here on Hispañola.

"While feasting greedily on the fish in the gourd, the four men panicked when they heard Yaya and his wife returning home for lunch" continued Mr. Badgyes.

"At that point Deminan Caracaracol, apparent leader of the gang, attempted to replace the container in the rafters when his

24. Taino *bohiques* (a type of healer/priest) treat smallpox patients.

25. Detail of a *bohique*.

26. Detail of the patient laying in a hammock. Hammocks were new inventions to the Europeans.

hold on the gourd broke causing it to crash to the ground."

"I was standing out in my front yard just minding my own business" recounted Inoscent Bistandyr, "when I heard a deafening roar. Suddenly my neighbor's front door burst open, spilling water willy-nilly. A great river, teeming with creatures of all shapes and sizes, rushed pell-mell across my lawn and took off toward the edge of town."

"Apparently when the gourd struck the ground, a flood gushed forth" interjected Katchin. "Now we're surrounded by water in vast quantities; it's rushing throughout the community and surrounding our land. Yep," pronounced Mr. Badgyes, "these boys are definitely going to be doing some serious community service in the future."

Small Hope

FOR SMALLPOX CURE

HISPANOLA, 1494

Yesterday, Mr. Stikoutyore Tungansayah, healer and priest of the largest of the five Taino kingdoms on Hispañola, somberly reported the first seven cases of a disease the white men call smallpox.

"This is not a good sign," worries Stikoutyore. "This disease is quite serious and extremely contagious. We may be in for quite an epidemic. And if it spreads," he continued looking anxious, "it's possible up to 80% of our population will be annihilated."

"I don't understand it" the healer lamented. "We Tainos endured a grueling migration from Venezuela ages ago and have been here on Hispañola since at least 1200 A.D. It's 1494 for crying out loud! We've survived hurricanes, Carib raiders, and even put canoes in the open ocean; you'd think we could cure just one little deadly disease, but this doesn't look good. Here's hoping we get a handle on it before it's too late."

THE NEWEST INVENTION FROM
ACROSS THE POND

BARNEY'S BARBECUES
YOU'LL NEVER BOIL FISH IN A POT AGAIN!

TIRED OF SOGGY FISH IN A BOWL?

Like your fish heads nice and crispy? Do you crave the flavor of wood smoke? Then cook your catch on one of Barney's Barbecues. Originally a Taino invention (they called it a "barabicu"), the barbecue eventually made its way north into Florida and the Carolinas, where John White recently caught the Secotan natives using it. Its simple construction, a grill raised above the fire on wooden sticks, makes it accessible to even the most inept chefs. It is sure to become a hit. Keep up with the Joneses and buy one of Barney's Barbecues today!

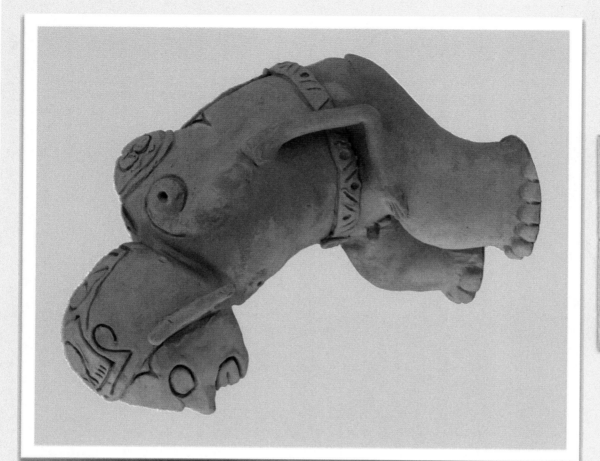

Forgery

Compare this artifact with the original on the left. Find ten differences.
Answers are on page 189.

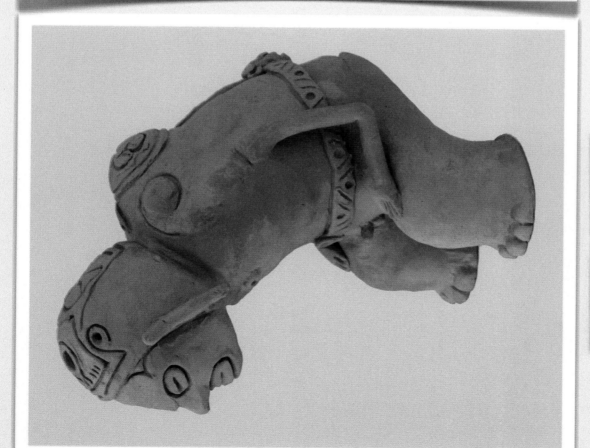

Original

Compare this artifact with the forgery on the right. Find ten differences.
Answers are on page 189.

ART FROM THE:
TAINO CULTURE
Bahamas, Greater Antilles, Lesser Antilles

BEGAN
c. 600 A.D.

CONTINUES
to present

Quadruplets Pardoned

In which we hear another old myth and learn why it's always good to have an axe on hand.

LEADER HAILED AS ARCHITECTURAL GENIUS

HISPANOLA, IN MYTHIC TIME

Questioned today for causing worldwide flooding, Deminan Caracaracol spilled the rest of the story to Sargent Yudebettr Telmithutrooth, of the Taino Police Department.

"After I dropped the gourd, my brothers and I were so panic-stricken that we ran helter-skelter to Grandfather Bayamanaco's house," exclaimed Deminan, "but a lot of help he was."

"The old man was quite incensed," agreed Sargent Telmithutrooth. "It seems that he had just made a culinary discovery, something called *cassava bread*, and wasn't interested in sharing his secret."

"I was just curious about the bread and that hot stuff that grandpa was cooking it over" whined Deminan, "so I asked for the recipe. And do you know what his answer was? I'll tell you! He spit at me! And as I spun around to avoid the loogie it hit me right between the shoulder blades."

"The story gets even stranger." interrupted Yudebettr. "By the time the police arrived,

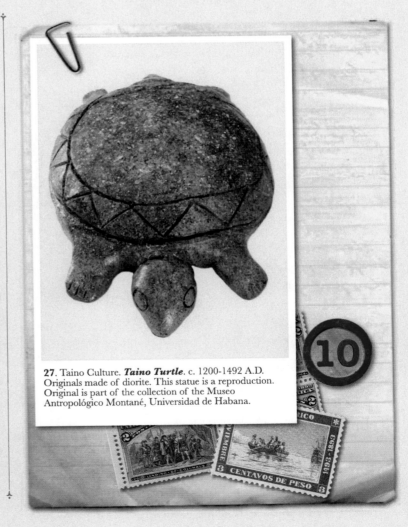

27. Taino Culture. ***Taino Turtle***. c. 1200-1492 A.D. Originals made of diorite. This statue is a reproduction. Original is part of the collection of the Museo Antropológico Montané, Universidad de Habana.

28. Jacques le Moyne (c. 1533-1588). *Florida Indians Storing Their Crops in the Public Granary.* Engraving.

the spittle on Deminan's back had become a massive, infected wound the size of a cantaloupe and he was near death! Imagine! From a wad of spit!"

"Then, before anyone could stop him," continued Telmithutrooth, "one of the quadruplets picked up an axe and split open Deminan's wound. Much to everyone's surprise a full-grown turtle popped out!"

"After the turtle emerged, we put the quadruplets into a squad cart and took them down to the station. Apparently the turtle inspired Deminan," Mr. Telmithutrooth answered. "because on the way to the station Deminan sketched a drawing of a hut with a turtle hoisted above as the roof. It was an inspiration: a domed roof just like the domed shell of the turtle."

"He insisted that from now on all Taino homes should be built in this manner. I was skeptical. After all, the sequence of events was just a little too surreal. Two hours before he was a juvenile delinquent and then suddenly he wanted us to believe he is the new Frank Lloyd Wright. The judge, however, was more sympathetic,"

concluded the sergeant. "He decided that in exchange for help erecting new homes around the island, Deminan and his brothers should be given their freedom. Who'd have guessed it would turn out so well?"

Cosmic Cover Causes Confusion

TATTLER CLARIFIES

HISPANOLA, IN MYTHIC TIME

A little confused by Deminan Caracaracol's turtle-on-the-roof thing, we here at the *Taino Tattler* tracked down someone to explain it to us.

TAINO HOUSES ARE SYMBOLIC

"It's really quite simple," stated Professor I.B. Smarht of the Taino Institute for Symbolic Studies. "Typically, Taino homes are round huts covered with a flat mat of grasses; Deminan proposes to change that. He wants to place a dome, shaped like the

The domed roof represents the dome of the heavens over our heads.

A DOME AWAY FROM DOME.

shell of a turtle, on top of the home to serve as a roof, similar to the public granary (figure 28)."

A MICROCOSM

"Symbolically this is a monumental change. With a domed roof, the average Taino home will now become a microcosm, a small representation of our cosmos, or universe."

"How does this new home represent the universe?" Smarht continued. "Our homes symbolize the earth. In them we live, sleep, eat and burn our cooking fires. The domed roof represents the heavens, the sky over our heads."

"This is nothing new. Many prehistoric cultures like ours have envisioned the sky as a dome. But raising a domed roof over each individual dwelling is absolutely brilliant!" Dr. Smarht explained.

"Because the smoke from each home fire will rise through the center of the roof to escape, each family will have a daily reminder that after death every soul will rise through the atmosphere and withdraw from the material universe. With this design everyday chores like cooking and heating become sacred rituals signifying meaningful events."

A MULTI-MEDIA PRESENTATION

"It's like an educational multi-media presentation replaying in each home every day!" Dr. Smarht said as he abruptly stopped and stared rather perplexedly out the window at nothing in particular. "Not that I have any idea what a multi-media presentation is," he concluded.

THERE'S NO PLACE LIKE DOME!

THAT LOOKS A LITTLE STRANGE IF YOU ASK ME.

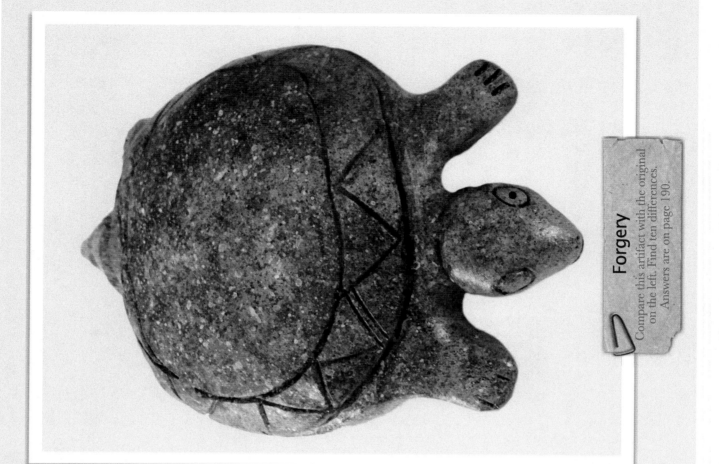

Forgery

Compare this artifact with the original on the left. Find ten differences. Answers are on page 190.

Original

Compare this artifact with the forgery on the right. Find ten differences. Answers are on page 189.

6
The Art of
John White

ROANOKE RABBLE

American Art History, Vol. No. 1   Bingo Card No. 11   artk12.com

AMERICAN ARTIST:
JOHN WHITE
London, Roanoke Colony

BORN
c. 1540

DIED
1593

Bizarre? Barbaric? Bah!

In which we learn that the Native Americans live boring lives just like us.

THERE'S NOTHING NEW UNDER THE SUN

ROANOKE, 1586

Nervous about the new world? Thinking about becoming a colonist? Worried about what you might find when you get there? Concerned that the inhabitants are less civilized than the typical Londoner? Good news! The newest evidence from across the pond suggests that native Virginians aren't barbarians at all!

Sure they don't wear much in the way of shirts and pants and they talk funny, but look on the bright side: they're town dwellers just like us. More importantly, their villages are small and barely defended. For potential colonists it doesn't get much better than that.

MEET JOHN WHITE, ARTIST

Where are we getting our information about the new land of Virginia you might ask? From a painting called the *The Indian Village of Pomeiock*, one of the 73 watercolors that artist John White painted while exploring the newly-discovered land in 1585.

Born in London sometime between 1540 and 1550, John White has become the first English artist to document the New World.

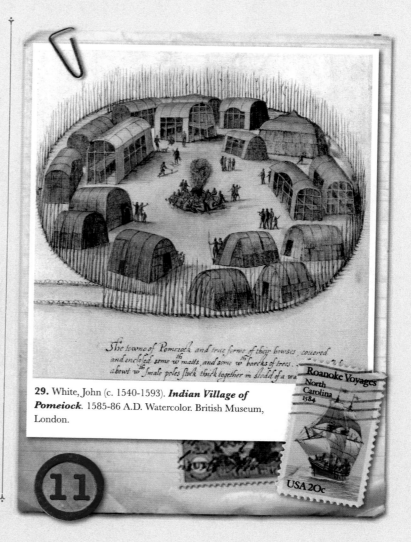

29. White, John (c. 1540-1593). ***Indian Village of Pomeiock***. 1585-86 A.D. Watercolor. British Museum, London.

30-32. White, John (c. 1540-1593). *Indian Village of Pomeiock* (detail). 1585-86 A.D. Watercolor. British Museum, London.

He traveled to Roanoke Island last year with Sir John Lane to document the land and its inhabitants. Now he is back helping to round up some adventurous souls to return to Roanoke and take a stab at colonization.

JOHN WHITE PAINTS THE TOWN RED

The first impression one receives from John's painting is that the village is well-built, neat and tidy. Pomeiock consists of eighteen buildings constructed of poles, mats and bark, each sporting an arched roof to keep the snow from collecting in the winter.

John even gives us glimpses of the inside of some of the homes. Each dwelling contains clean, well-swept floors and raised benches built into the side walls. How civilized of them, they don't sleep on the floor.

MEET THE NATIVE VIRGINIANS

What about the villagers? What do we know about them? Are they barbaric? Boorish? Brutal? Do they eat babies and kittens? According to this document, the answer is definitely "no."

Apparently they do pretty much the same boring things we do. Mr. White shows them walking about the village, splitting wood, sitting around a fire and returning from the hunt. We even see uncooked children and a dog.

WORRIED ABOUT SAFETY?

What about their defenses? Is their town protected? Is it surrounded by an impenetrable stone wall, iron gates, or maybe a moat? Nope, just a flimsy palisade; nothing a few axes and a little gun powder couldn't handle, if necessary.

A HOME AWAY FROM HOME

So if you're thinking about hauling your tuckus across the Atlantic to confront the new world, haul away. Thanks to John White's documentation you can rest assured that even though it's a highly populated land, it's neither bizarre nor barbaric. You might even want to call it home.

"The towne of Pomeiock and true forme of their howses, covered and enclosed some with matts and some with barcks of trees. All compassed abowt with smale poles stock thick together in stedd of a wall."

-John White's text at the bottom of *The Town of Pomeiock* (original spelling uncorrected)

CLEAN UP! PAGE 63! WAMPUM BEADS FROM CHAPTER 4!

PETE'S PALISADES

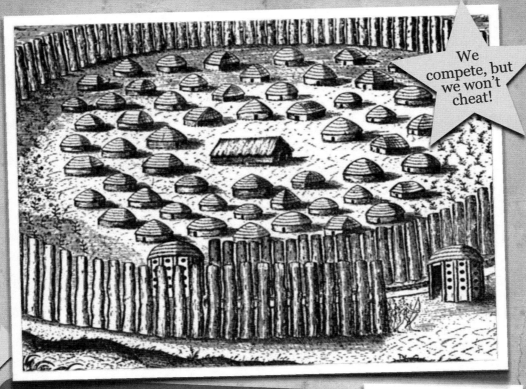

We compete, but we won't cheat!

NEED A FENCE?

TIRED OF FENDING OFF WOLVES AT NIGHT? NEED TO KEEP THOSE PESKY COLONISTS AT BAY? HIDE YOURSELF BEHIND ONE OF PETE'S PALISADES. DON'T KNOW WHAT A PALISADE IS? IT'S A PROTECTIVE FENCE MADE OF POINTY WOODEN POLES. THEY'RE ALL THE RAGE IN NORTH AMERICA AND **NO ONE BUILDS THEM BETTER THAN PETE!**

Safeguard your loved ones
TODAY!

Original

Compare this painting with the forgery below. Find ten differences. Answers are on page 190.

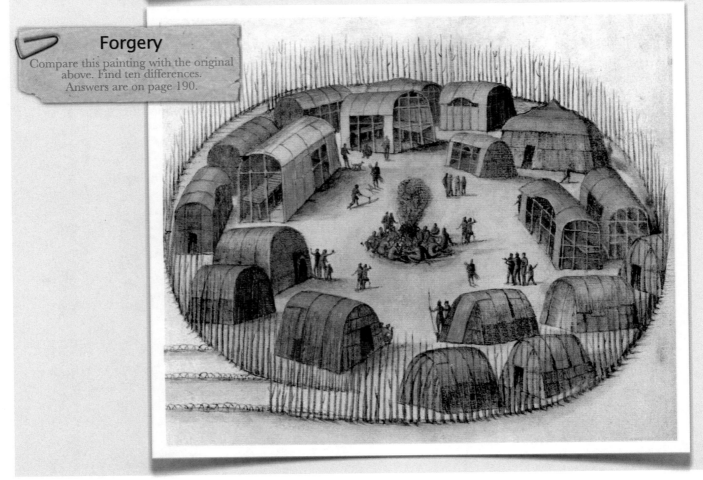

Forgery

Compare this painting with the original above. Find ten differences. Answers are on page 190.

JOHN WHITE, ILLUSTRATOR

Going on an expedition of discovery?

Need to document new species of plants and animals? Want to entice new people to your colony? Hire John White to illustrate, design, and sketch his way into your enterprise.

Hire John once and you'll want him back again and again!

John is such a talented artist that representing many of Roanoke's species of fish was no problem at all. He is an illustrator extraordinaire.

Impress your clients with John's impeccable perspective. Take a look at the way he draws the weir in *Indians Fishing*. What's a weir? It's like a giant fence in the water to corral the fish. Notice how the three-dimensional effect allows it to recede into the distance.

Like a squirrel stuffing nuts in a hollow tree, John has crammed a boatload of information into one painting. Here, he includes four methods of fishing in one illustration: spear fishing, night fishing, weir fishing, and net fishing. John's pictures are truly worth a thousand words.

33. White, John (c. 1540-1593). *Indians Fishing.* 1585-86 A.D. Watercolor. British Museum, London.

No smoke and mirrors here! John can help you tell it like it is. He doesn't embellish or exaggerate. For example, the Algonquin natives really do make fires in the bottom of their boats. But they're not just blowing smoke, they're night fishing. The firelight attracts the fish and then whammo! They're breakfast.

Have bigger fish to fry? John can do more than paint. He's adept at noticing and recording cutting-edge inventions as well. At the center of *Indians Fishing* is a new type of boat that he has labeled a *cannow*. Natives create these *cannows* by hollowing out large tree trunks.

So if you need something documented, illustrated, narrated or detailed, be sure to hire John White. It's like having a living, breathing, camera (whatever that is) at your disposal.

COME TO
DREW & STU'S!
And buy some canoes!

SALE
Buy one canoe and
get two oars, FREE!

DREW & STU'S
DUGOUT CANOES

Have you been fruitlessly pummeling the base of a tree with a stone axe? Do you need dependable water transportation but don't have any iron or copper tools? Drew & Stu have a solution for you! Let us chop down a tree for you and turn it into one of our famous dugout canoes using only stone tools.

Yes, you heard right: only stone tools! What's our secret? Fire! We harness fire to help with each stage of the process. Experienced lumberjacks burn around the base of the trunk to help chop the tree down. Then talented craftsmen burn off excess limbs. Finally, experienced artisans burn and scrape the wood from the core of the trunk. We spare no steps to make your canoe the finest available.

Come to Drew & Stu's Dugout Canoes TODAY!

34. De Bry, Theodor (engraver, 1528-1598) after John White (original artist, c. 1540-1593). *Indians Making Canoes*. 1590 A.D. Engraving.

Forgery

Compare this painting with the original on the left. Find ten differences. Answers are on page 190.

The manner of their fishing.

Original

Compare this painting with the forgery on the right. Find ten differences. Answers are on page 189.

The manner of their fishing.

7
The Art of Early Virginia

VIRGINIA REVIEW

AMERICAN ART FROM THE:
POWHATAN CULTURE
Virginia area, USA

BEGAN
date unknown

CONTINUES
to present

American Art History, Vol. No. 1   Bingo Card No. 13   artk12.com

Powhatan Steals the Scene

In which we learn what threads Pocahontas' father dons when he's dressed for success.

CHIC CHIEF USHERS IN NEW FASHION FAD

VIRGINIA, 1600 AD

What will the well-dressed Algonquian chief be wearing this season? If the fashion world follows Powhatan's lead it will be mantles, mantles, mantles.

WHAT IS A MANTLE?

It's a cloak, a cape, a cover for your carcass. But we're not talking about any old rags you might throw on to go check the rabbit snares in the rain. We're referring to ceremonial suits, dignified duds, regal robes. In other words, a mantle is a fashion statement.

MEANINGFUL DESIGNS

A mantle should be adorned with meaningful designs to suit each individual chief. Stitched

35. Algonquian Native American Artisans. ***Powhatan's Mantle***. c. 1600. Deer hide, shells and sinew, 63 x 102 in. Ashmolean Museum of Art and Archaeology, University of Oxford, England (Part of the Tradescant Collection).

THE STORY OF POCAHONTAS

13

Do you lack a sense of style? Want to dress for success?

RIDE THE FASHION WAVE HANGING ON TO POWHATAN'S COAT-TAILS

together from four deer hides to accommodate even the largest frame, *Powhatan's Mantle* sports a silhouette of himself flanked by his two totem animals, all painstakingly stitched in shell beads.

PARTNERS IN THE PATTERN

Scattered around the rest of the cape are 34 solid-beaded circles each representing a loyal village in his growing confederacy. The effect screams power and prestige. Come this fall, all eyes will be on the chief who dares to don such smart threads.

Rumor has it that Powhatan will display his dignified drapery soon when the foreigner, Captain John Smith, visits for his trial. When it comes to fashion, emulate the best! Update your wardrobe today.

King Powhatan comands C.Smith to be slayne his daughter Pokahontas beggs his life his thankfullnefs and how he Subiected 39 of their kings riade y history

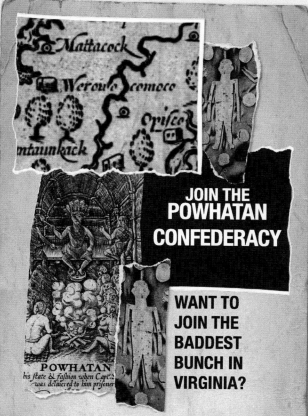

POWHATAN
his state & fashion when Capt. was delivered to him prisoner

Forgery

Compare this artifact with the original on the left. Find ten differences. Answers are on page 190.

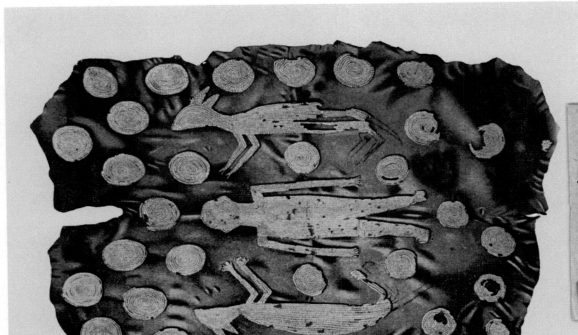

Original

Compare this artifact with the forgery on the right. Find ten differences. Answers are on page 189.

VIRGINIA REVIEW

American Art History, Vol. No. 1   Bingo Card No. 14   artk12.com

AMERICAN ARTIST:
JOHN SMITH
London, Jamestown Colony

BORN
1580

DIED
JUNE 21, 1631

A Voice Crying Out in the Wilderness

In which we learn that the New World isn't new, the wilderness isn't wild and that Virginia doesn't come in a shrink-wrapped box.

SAYS IT ISN'T SO WILD AFTER ALL

VIRGINIA, 1613 AD

The word "wilderness" conjures up all sorts of vacant images: barren badlands, desolate deserts, and forsaken forests. This is how most explorers have described the new world of North America. In fact, even that term "new" brings to mind sparkling blue waters and dewy greenery in an untrodden landscape trussed up in shrink wrap like a box of chocolates on St. Valentine's Day.

But Captain John Smith of the Virginia Company has recently discovered that that the word "wilderness" is about as appropriate for describing Virginia as the word "cuddly" is for describing an electric eel.

Mr. Smith has exposed this inconvenient

36. Smith, John. *Virginia, Discovered and Discribed by Captayn John Smith* (sixth state). [London: William Hole] 1624. Engraved map, 32 1/4 x 46 1/4". Library of Congress, Washington D.C. (Purchase, The Alfred N. Punnett Endowment Fund and George D. Pratt Gift, 1934).

It is teeming with tenants, brimming with burgs, swarming with cities and heaped with hamlets.

DO I MAKE MYSELF CLEAR?

truth in his recently published *Map of Virginia* where he documents not only the lay of the land, but also the status of its citizenry. It's populated, folks. And we're not just talking about an occasional hut or longhouse scattered among the shrubbery. According to Smith's map it is teeming with tenants, brimming with burgs, swarming with cities and heaped with hamlets. Do I make myself clear?

Just in the Chesapeake Bay region alone, Smith records over 200 native towns and villages. In fact, the natives call this region Tsenacommacah, which means "densely-inhabited land."

And it's not just a hodgepodge of unrelated tents and huts like a KOA campground in the middle of downtown London; it's sophisticated. Some towns have chiefs, and some don't; some are allied, and some aren't. There are towns, villages, temples, hunting grounds, fishing rights, and a giant confederacy that encompasses it all.

So if you think you're going to waltz in there and claim a plot of land like it's a new subdivision then you're in for a surprise. It's occupied. And staking a claim is going to take more than a fancy piece of paper; it's going to take some fancy negotiating or some fancy fighting or both.

So if you're thinking about making a claim, study John's map, because it *will* be a wild ride, but it *won't* be in the wilderness.

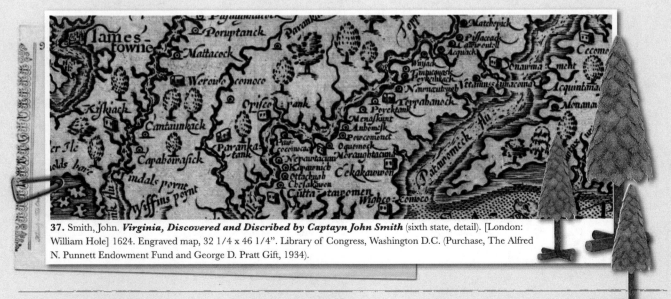

37. Smith, John. ***Virginia, Discovered and Discribed by Captayn John Smith*** (sixth state, detail). [London: William Hole] 1624. Engraved map, 32 1/4 x 46 1/4". Library of Congress, Washington D.C. (Purchase, The Alfred N. Punnett Endowment Fund and George D. Pratt Gift, 1934).

JOHN SMITH'S *MAP OF VIRGINIA*

Setting out to explore the Chesapeake bay region? Hoping to find riches in the New World? Think you can discover a water route to the Pacific? Before you try, buy John Smith's *Map of Virginia*.

John undertook 20 separate trips and traveled over 2500 miles to produce a map of extraordinary accuracy and quality. Using only a compass, a quadrant, and information from knowledgeable natives, John has seamlessly melded together geographical features with cultural information to help guide you through rough and unfamiliar territory.

Fearless soldier, intrepid explorer, author, and cartographer, John Smith (right) has seen and done it all. He singlehandedly rescued the Jamestown colony from self-destruction and was, in turn, rescued by Pocahontas when her father Powhatan threatened to behead him.

Feeling social? John has labeled over 200 native towns from large to small. To keep you from looking like a tourist he has labeled them with their native names spelled phonetically in English. Visit Powhatan's home town, Weromecomoco (bottom, middle left) on a Saturday night and see what the chief and his cronies do for fun.

The *Map of Virginia* highlights the Chesapeake Bay area and labels all other major bays, shorelines, rivers, tributaries, and islands. Included among the geographic features is the tiny European outpost called Jamestown (bottom, far right).

A rare glimpse of the inside of a native house (left) opens up on the top left side of the map. This illustration shows Powhatan presiding over a group of men at a council meeting. John's caption states, "Powhatan held this state and fashion when Captain Smith was delivered to him prisoner, 1607." Apparently this event didn't terrify Smith so much that he couldn't take notes for a future drawing.

Ready to meet the neighbors? The Susquehannock warrior (left, BELOW) belongs to a group that lives at the northern end of Virginia. John comments "The Sasquesahanougs are a giant-like people and thus atyred." If the "giant" comment doesn't make you shake and sweat, the variety of pelts on his uniform will.

This handy key (bottom, right) helps the viewer navigate through the new territory. Need to find a person of authority? Locate a village marked by a "king's howse" and you will find a chief living there. Want to visit a smaller village? Just look for a town marked by an "ordinary howse." John even lets you know when he's out of his league. He marks with crosses villages that he's only heard of, but not personally visited.

Discovered and described by Captain John Smith
Graven by William Hole 1606

At the bottom of the map, John writes, "Discovered and discribed by Captain John Smith. Graven by William Hole, 1606." Don't let the date confuse you. John knows that Jamestown was founded in 1607; he was there. The date on the map reads 1606 because that is the year that the Virginia Company issued the charter.

Signification of these markes,
To the crosses hath bin discouerd
what beyond is by relation ☩
Kings howses 2 ____
Ordinary howses 2 ____ o

W A N T E D

Cutting-Edge Company Courting Courageous Characters

Are you an adventuresome animal? A daring dude? A spunky specimen? Do you radiate recklessness? Manifest moxie? Percolate pluck? Are you fed up with life in London? Are you an aristocrat without a future? Are you wiling to leave it all behind? If so, consider coming on board with the Virginia Company. We offer challenging futures for fearless fellows in Jamestown and Plymouth. If interested carry your carcass down to the wharf and sign on. No experience necessary. Armor and weapons a plus.

Make King James proud. Join our company today!

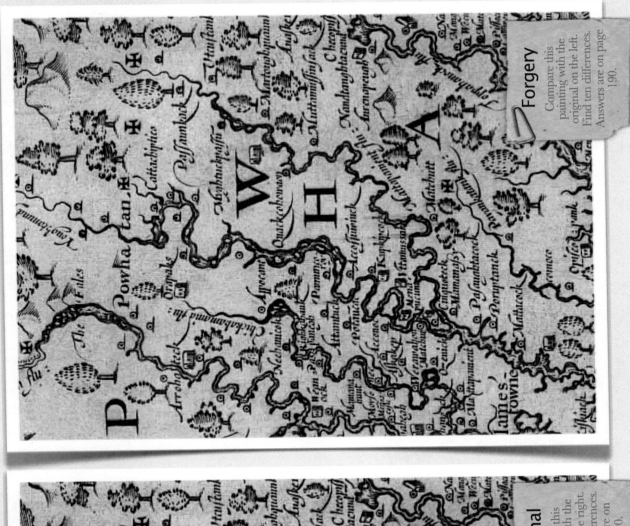

Forgery

Compare this painting with the original on the left. Find ten differences. Answers are on page 190.

Original

Compare this painting with the forgery on the right. Find ten differences. Answers are on page 190.

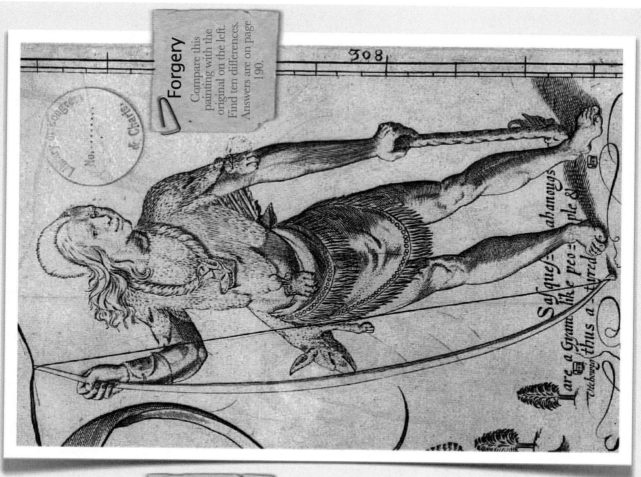

Forgery

Compare this painting with the original on the left. Find ten differences. Answers are on page 190.

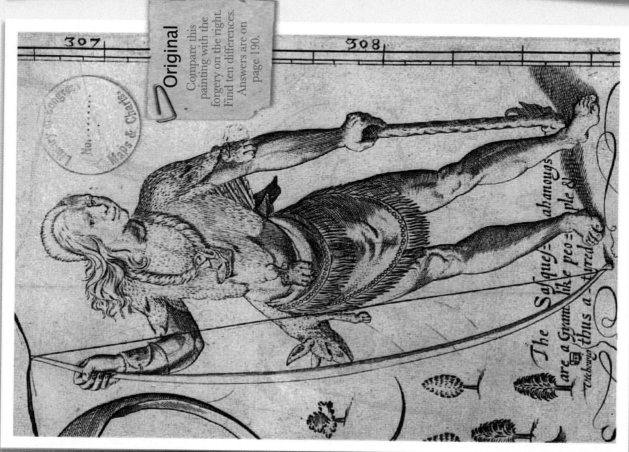

Original

Compare this painting with the forgery on the right. Find ten differences. Answers are on page 190.

Forgery

Compare this painting with the original on the left. Find ten differences. Answers are on page 190.

Original

Compare this painting with the forgery on the right. Find ten differences. Answers are on page 190.

8
Early
Colonial
Portraiture

AMERICAN ARTIST:
THE FREAKE PAINTER
Massachusetts, USA

BORN
date unknown

DIED
date unknown

Flat Is Where It's At

In which we learn why being roadkill is good and why casting shadows is bad.

WANNA BE HIP? BE FLAT.

BOSTON, 1675

After taking a look at some of his work, Tritoo Impressmie, expert art critic here at the *Boston Babbler*, draws some interesting conclusions about the artist they call the Freake painter.

"He's good," judges Tritoo, "maybe even great. Lay people may take one look at his portraits of Mr. and Mrs. Freake and conclude that he is a hack, a piker, or a greenhorn. They might say that because the people in his works appear flat instead of three-dimensional that he is just a beginner and an uneducated one at that. It's simply not true. The Freake painter knows exactly what he is doing and why he is doing it."

ELIZABETHAN STYLE

"He is employing a style called the Elizabethan style," Tritoo continues, "an approach to painting that began in England under Queen Elizabeth and ended with King James. With this technique, the goal is to make the people in the portrait appear flat. To give a piece of

HOW DOES MY HAIR LOOK, HONEY?

38. Freake Painter. ***John Freake***. c. 1671. Oil on canvas, 42 x 36 3/4". Worcester Art Museum, Worcester, Massachusetts (Sarah C. Garver Fund, 1963.135).

15

16

HONESTLY, IT LOOKS KIND OF FLAT.

39. Freake Painter. *Elizabeth Clarke Freake (Mrs. John Freake) and Baby Mary*. c. 1671 and 1674. Oil on canvas, 42 1/2 x 36 3/4". Worcester Art Museum, Worcester, Massachusetts (Gift of Mr. and Mrs. Albert W. Rice, 1963.134).

40. Hillard, Nicolas. *Queen Elizabeth I (The Phoenix Portrait)*. 1575. Oil on wood, 31 1/8 x 24 in. National Portrait Gallery, London.

art the illusion of three dimensions, artists typically add shadows and perspective; the Elizabethan style avoids both."

"For kings, queens and aristocrats, shadows and perspective are too mundane," continues Mr. Impressmie. "They are part of the common world, something the riffraff have to deal with. Eliminating those techniques elevates the subject of the portrait above the common world."

"Queen Elizabeth summed it up best when she told her court painter that she wanted her portrait to be painted without shadows because shadows made her look too real, too common, too much a part of the everyday world. Elizabeth felt superior, majestic, elevated above the ordinary, and wanted her portrait to reflect it. After all, she was royalty and royalty had to keep their distance."

"Like many upper-class Americans," notes Mr. Impressmie, "the Freakes have similar, though more subdued, delusions of grandeur."

PROSPERITY AND STATUS

"Let's examine their portraits more closely" suggests Tritoo. "Mr. Freake's gloves and intricate lace collar reveal that he is a wealthy gentleman and merchant. Mrs. Freake's lace, her exquisite fabrics, and the expensive chair that she sits upon also attest to the family's prosperity and status."

"Mr. Freake certainly looks rather proud and self-satisfied, and that's what seventeenth-century Elizabethan-style portraits represent: esteem, honor, influence, and plenty of moolah."

ROMAN AND MEDIEVAL ROOTS

"Though this style seems a bit superficial and pretentious, or 'hifalutin,' as my mother used to say, the purpose of the original two-dimensional portrait was far from shallow" assures Mr. Impressmie. "The style can be traced back at least as far as late Roman and Early Medieval times."

"In later Roman times artists painted portraits on wooden panels and placed

AHHHH! A SHADOW! MY CARD IS CASTING A SHADOW!

Emotionless faces and shadowless bodies remind the viewer that we are looking at souls who live in a spiritual domain.

them on wrapped mummies to give the dead identities for eternity. These portraits are relatively flat with large staring eyes to emphasize the individual's spirituality, because in those days eyes were considered to be windows to the soul."

"Medieval icons borrowed some of the same symbolism. On these panels, Jesus, the Virgin Mary, His disciples, and many saints all display expressionless faces and little or no shadows to remind the viewer that we are looking at a soul who lives in a spiritual domain, outside the realm where émotions and shadows exist."

SPIRITUAL HERITAGE

"Even though Elizabethan portraits are now little more than a fashion statement, they do retain a little of their spiritual heritage. In their portraits the Freakes are easily identifiable as Puritans, and this is intentional. For Puritans, wealth and prosperity are symbols of God's favor and blessings. According to Puritan philosophy, if you are wealthy that means you must be a good Christian. These portraits symbolize that belief."

"Of course there is some unmistakeable irony here," concludes Tritoo. "Christians are supposed to be humble. Plastering your success on a canvas for all to see kind of negates that. But hey, if

you want to advertise your accomplishments, what better way to puff yourself up than to be flat?"

41. Unknown Artist. *Portrait of a Young Woman in Red*. c. 90-120 A.D. Encaustic, lime wood, gilding, 15 x 7 1/4 in. Metropolitan Museum of Art, New York (Rogers Fund,

42. Unknown Artist. *Portrait of a Man with a Mole on his Nose*. c. 130-150 A.D. Encaustic, lime wood, 15 1/2 x 7 5/8 in. Metropolitan Museum of Art, New York (Rogers Fund, 1909).

43. Unknown Artist. *Icon of Saint George*. c. 1300s A.D. Byzantine and Christian Museum, Athens, Greece.

Photoshopping is Fashionable

FREAKES FIT FINAL FAMILY MEMBER INTO PORTRAIT

BOSTON, 1675 AD

"I wouldn't call it *photoshopping*. I don't reckon I've ever heard that word before, but yes, originally when Elizabeth and I had our portraits painted in 1671 it was just the two of us," comments Mr. John Freake, local attorney and merchant. "When our eighth child, Mary, came along in 1674 the artist returned at our request and added her in."

"Originally my wife held a fan in one hand. The artist painted over the fan and moved her arms. Then he reduced the puffiness of her sleeves so you can see more of the expensive chair she is sitting in. (All this was done, of course, with the utmost skill. You can't tell that any changes have been made at all.) Finally, the painter added the babe and *Voila!*" concludes John, "Baby Mary is immortalized forever."

Painter Freake: Is He a Geek?

ARTIST SADDLED WITH LAMENTABLE LABEL

BOSTON, 1675 AD

The short answer is, of course, no; the Freake painter is not a geek. In all probability he was normal and well-respected. He is, most likely, a man, (very few painters are women here in the seventeenth century) and by examining the style and quality of his portraits, experts conclude that a total of ten paintings exist that are attributed to his hand, and they are all of excellent quality. He is, by most standards, an accomplished painter.

Then why the weird moniker? No one knows his true identity; when artists are unknown the art world names the unidentified artist after one of his most well-known works. Unfortunately for Mr. Anonymous, his most well-known pieces are the Freake portraits. Therefore he becomes the Freake painter. Our deepest sympathies, sir.

44. Freake Painter. ***Elizabeth Clarke Freake (Mrs. John Freake) and Baby Mary*** (detail). c. 1671 and 1674. Oil on canvas, 42 1/2 x 36 3/4". Worcester Art Museum, Worcester, Massachusetts (Gift of Mr. and Mrs. Albert W. rice, 1963.134).

45. Freake Painter. ***John Freake*** (detail). c. 1671. Oil on canvas, 42 x 36 3/4". Worcester Art Museum, Worcester, Massachusetts (Sarah C. Garver Fund, 1963.135).

46. Freake Painter. ***Elizabeth Clarke Freake (Mrs. John Freake) and Baby Mary*** (detail). c. 1671 and 1674. Oil on canvas, 42 1/2 x 36 3/4". Worcester Art Museum, Worcester, Massachusetts (Gift of Mr. and Mrs. Albert W. rice, 1963.134).

W A N T E D

3D Person Seeking 2D Portrait

Wealthy, devoted, well-dressed, Puritan gentleman seeks skilled, European-trained painter to immortalize him on canvas. Must be able to paint in the Elizabethan style with no deep shadows and very little perspective. Must be able to illustrate fancy lace, buttons, cloth and hair in exquisite detail. Must provide own brushes and canvas. Broad color palette required. Can pay in pounds or local currency. If interested please provide references.

Forgery

Compare this painting with the original on the left. Find ten differences. Answers are on page 191.

Original

Compare this painting with the forgery on the right. Find ten differences. Answers are on page 191.

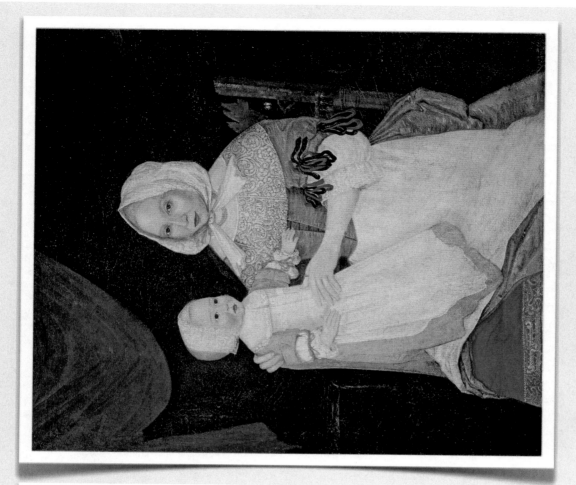

Forgery

Compare this painting with the original on the left. Find ten differences.
Answers are on page 191.

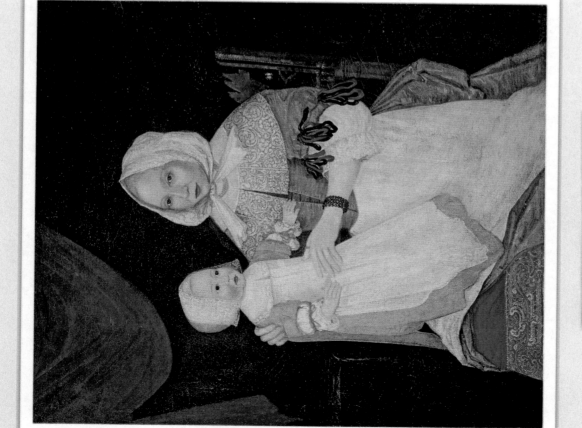

Original

Compare this painting with the forgery on the right. Find ten differences.
Answers are on page 191.

AMERICAN ARTIST:
CAPTAIN THOMAS SMITH
Massachusetts, USA

BORN
date unknown

DIED
date unknown

Somber Self-Portrait

CRITICS SHED SOME LIGHT

In which we learn very little about Captain Thomas Smith.

BOSTON, C. 1750 AD

Mr. Nohzinthuh Ayer, Boston's premier art critic, dropped by the *Boston Babbler* this week to give us an exclusive interview interpreting the *Self-Portrait of Captain Thomas Smith,* the first known self-portrait painted in the American colonies.

BABBLER: Thank you for coming Mr. Ayer. Glad to have you here with us today.

AYER: I'm sure you are.

BABBLER: Right. Um, tell us about this piece of art.

AYER: Well, to begin with it's an "emblematic" work, though I doubt you have any idea what that means.

BABBLER: Ah, you mean symbolic, metaphorical, that things in the painting stand for something beyond what they physically represent?

AYER: Quite.

BABBLER: So give us a few examples. What's emblematic in Captain Thomas' self-portrait?

AYER: To begin with, the drapery behind him, his chair, and his lace collar are all emblematic. Because these items were

47. Smith, Captain Thomas. ***Self-Portrait***. c. 1690. Oil on canvas, 24.4 x 23.6 in. Worcester Art Museum, Worcester, Massachusetts.

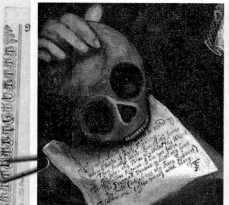

48-49. Smith, Captain Thomas. *Self-Portrait* (details). c. 1690. Oil on canvas, 24.4 x 23.6 in. Worcester Art Museum, Worcester, Massachusetts.

very expensive we can assume that he included them in his portrait to say that he was rather affluent, wealthy, not part of the common riffraff.

BABBLER: Hmmm. Which Thomas Smith are we referring to? There were about fourteen Thomas Smiths in Boston during his time. The name was rather, uh, *common*.

AYER: Unfortunately we don't really know; we presume he was one of the wealthy ones.

BABBLER: So you know who the artist of the self-portrait was, but you don't really know who he was.

AYER: You could put it that way, if you must.

BABBLER: We must. Continue please. What else in the painting is emblematic?

AYER: Well, the window in the background shows a rather involved naval battle.

BABBLER: That sounds interesting. Tell us more.

AYER: Regrettably. That's all we know.

BABBLER: Too bad. What does it symbolize?

AYER: Well, the battle symbolizes the struggles of his life and of life in general.

BABBLER: He was a naval captain?

AYER: We assume, but we don't know for sure.

BABBLER: How awkward. What about the skull; what does it represent?

AYER: Rather obvious, don't you think? It symbolizes death: his death, your death, my death, the inevitable death of the human race. That's why he is touching it. He's admitting that he, like everyone else, is mortal and will one day die. The poem beneath the skull supports that theory.

BABBLER: How did Captain Thomas die?

AYER: No clue. Though if he worked for this paper most likely of boredom.

BABBLER: Er, yeah, well, Nohz, thank you for sparing us some of your time today; it was rather, um, enlightening.

AYER: Of course it was.

AND I THOUGHT THAT I WAS THE ONLY ONE WHO LIKED SKULLS.

BOSTON BARDS
POETRY READING

FEATURING THE WORK OF CAPTAIN THOMAS SMITH

WEDNESDAY EVENING		ENTRY FEE
7PM		**FREE**

Why why should I the world be minding

therein a World of Evils Finding.

Then Farwell World; Farwell they Jarres

thy Joies thy Toies thy Wiles thy Warrs

Truth Sounds Retreat: I am not sorye.

The Eternal Drawes to him my heart

By Faith (which can thy Force Subvert)

To Crowne me (after Grace) with Glory.

DON'T MISS IT!

FEATURING HIS POEM SHOWCASED ⟶ BENEATH THE SKULL IN HIS PORTRAIT

KEEP IN MIND SPELLING IS UNIMPORTANT HERE IN THE SEVENTEENTH CENTURY

9
The Art of Matthew Pratt

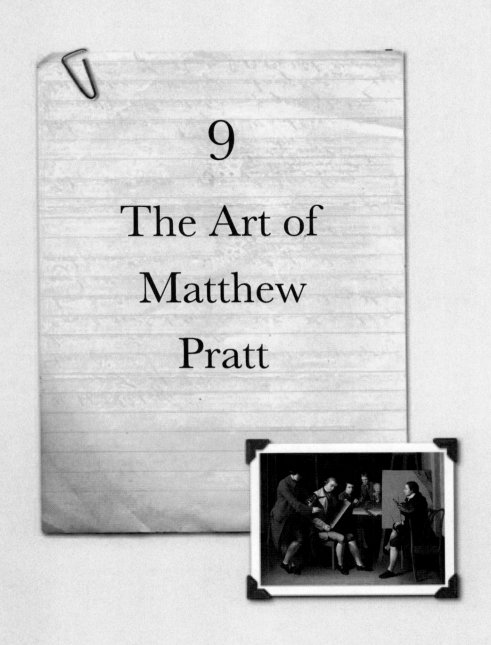

AMERICAN ARTIST:
MATTHEW PRATT
Philadelphia, PA

BORN
September 23, 1834

DIED
January 9, 1903

For *The American School* Matthew Pratt Gets Good Marks

In which we take a peek inside an eighteenth-century art studio and learn where to get a good Philly cheesesteak sandwich.

MATTHEW PRATT SHOWS AND TELLS

LONDON, LATE IN 1765

This weekend the Society of Artists of Great Britain are hosting an exhibition. We here at the *Philadelphia Feature* sent our foreign correspondent, Mr. Ahrwee Thairyett to England several weeks ago to cover the event.

THE AMERICAN SCHOOL

"One of the most significant paintings on display this weekend, at least from the colonial point of view, is Matthew Pratt's *The American School,*" reports Mr. Thairyett. "Sure, it's a blatant advertisement for Mr. Pratt's portrait business, but beyond that, it promises to mark a critical moment in the development of colonial American art."

INSIDE AN ART STUDIO

"I'll start from the beginning." begins Ahrwee. "This painting shows the inside of an idealized art studio and illustrates the process of a student becoming a full-fledged painter."

STEP ONE

"The younger boys at the back of the table, the ones in the blue and green suits,

50. Pratt, Matthew (1734-1805). *The American School*. 1765. Oil on canvas, 36 x 50 1/4 in. The Metropolitan Museum of Art, New York City, New York.

HEY, LOOK AT THESE COOL SKETCHES OF PETER RABBIT I JUST MADE; HE'S WEARING A REBEL UNIFORM AND SHOOTING A CANNON AT SOME BRITISH SOLDIERS.

51-52. Pratt, Matthew (1734-1805). ***The American School*** (detail).1765. Oil on canvas, 36 x 50 1/4 in. The Metropolitan Museum of Art, New York City, New York.

demonstrate the first step in an artist's education: copying master drawings, and drawing plaster casts.

Beginning artists practice drawing by imitating the masters. In doing so they often copy lithographs or other prints of paintings and drawings. These are represented by the folder and the stack of prints that the young boy in the green suit holds.

Another method of teaching the art of drawing require students to draw from reproductions of famous sculpture; these reproductions are called plaster casts. The boy in the blue suit sketches the cast of a young boy on the table in front of him.

STEP TWO

The older student in the grey suit represents the next step: drawing from life, though there is no live model visible in the painting.

THE END RESULT

The man at the easel, Pratt himself, represents the finished product of this educational process. After spending years drawing from prints, casts, and live models the student paints portraits in full color. By seating himself at an easel holding a palette of oil paints, Pratt shows himself a master of the final step. In other words, the painting is his diploma. He is finished.

The American School is also Pratt's visual resumé. It is on display at the Society as a sort of eighteenth-century billboard advertising both his skill and availability. However, the entire painting is a fabrication. His "resumé" is a lie. Although this painting illustrates the proper training for well-bred artists, it is a training that Pratt never received.

Matthew Pratt grew up in Philadelphia, received a typical academic education, and at fifteen apprenticed to his Uncle Phil where he learned to paint portraits, business signs, and in a pinch, houses. In fact, one of his most celebrated signs is visible over the Cock-in-a-Barnyard Beer House on Spruce Street here in Philly. They serve some of the best cheesesteak sandwiches in town, but I digress. Matthew's education was

YO! SOMEONE LEFT THEIR BRUSHES ON PAGE 99!

American artists are no longer just amateurs painting tavern signs and memorializing Aunt Irma's prize-winning hog.

not an elite education, but it served his needs.

THE MASTER

The last man in the painting is the master of the studio; he wears a green suit and stands with his face in shadow. To represent the master Pratt chose none other than Philadelphia's own, celebrated Benjamin West.

In 1764, at the age of thirty, Pratt traveled to England and spent four years living and working with Benjamin West at his studio. Although Matthew could claim the honor of being one of Benjamin West's first "students" from the colonies, he does not. According to Pratt, he and West are equals. In this painting he does not claim to be his student; he is "name dropping." This is "fame by association." West is a well-respected artist from the colonies and by including him on his resumé Pratt makes a good business move.

WHAT'S THE POINT?

So why is this painting significant for the colonies? Why did I travel three months over choppy Atlantic waters just to be able to talk about five guys in funky suits scribbling on boards and playing with paint? Well, Matthew's timing is fortuitous and his painting is important. It signifies a new level of artistic quality in the Colonies.

On one level his painting titled *The American School* refers to the practical training of a master artist. On another level it refers to the artists born here in the colonies, American artists.

American artists are no longer just amateurs painting tavern signs, and memorializing Aunt Irma's prize-winning hog. Some, are truly professional painters and can rival the best Europe has to offer.

As if on cue, Pratt finishes a painting titled *The American School* just as the artists from the American Colonies seem to be coming into their own. And just as Pratt finishes the painting titled *The American School*, there actually is an American School, a growing list of artists who can compete with the European School, artists like Benjamin West, John Singleton Copley, Gilbert Stuart, and Charles Willson Peale It is a monumental turning point in the history American art.

Unfortunately, however, though he admires the talent of other American artists, Pratt overvalues his own. His skills are not equal to the best America has to offer; his portraits will not go down in the annals of history with the elite. But because it marks such an historic moment in the history of art, *The American School* will.

HEY!

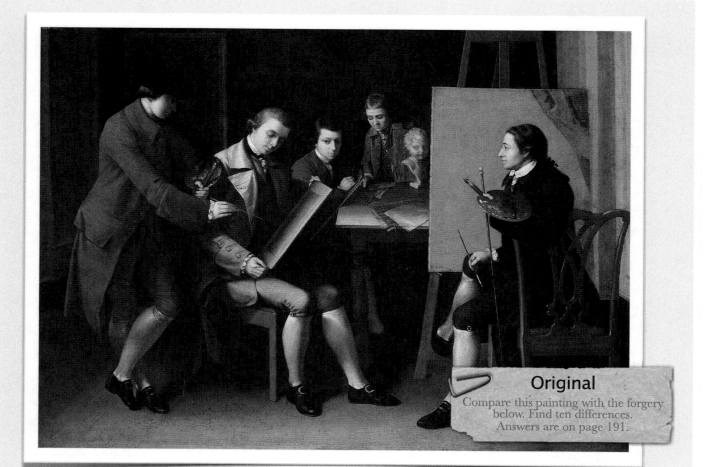

Original

Compare this painting with the forgery below. Find ten differences.
Answers are on page 191.

Forgery

Compare this painting with the original above. Find ten differences.
Answers are on page 191.

10
Spanish
Colonial
Architecture

SPANISH SPEWER

American Art History, Vol. No. 1   Bingo Card No. 19   artk12.com

AMERICAN ART:
SPANISH COLONIAL ARCHITECTURE
North America

BEGAN
1521

ENDED
1821

Remember the Alamo?

In which we learn the original purpose of the Alamo and why aliens should never wear Elvis costumes.

THE SPANISH COLONIZE TEXAS

SAN ANTONIO, TEXAS, PRESENT DAY

Ey Mizpoke, popular reporter here at the Spanish Spewer, employs his offbeat and unedited method of journalism to give us a new look at an old building.

A SPANISH MISSION

The image of the Alamo usually brings to mind James Bowie, Santa Ana, ~~Elvis Presley~~ (I mean) Davy Crockett, and the battle that took place there in 1836, but the Alamo has a history that stretches back long before that date.

The Alamo is a mission. A mission is a kind of religious outpost built by the Spanish Catholic Church in the Americas between 1521-1821. The Spanish Empire built missions to colonize ~~Antarctica~~ (I mean) North and South America. Historians call the architecture that the Spanish built during this period "Spanish Colonial Architecture."

After Columbus arrived in the Caribbean, Spain conquered most of the Americas including Mexico, the Southern United States, Central America and parts of South America. Spain

53. *Mission San Antonio de Valero (The Alamo)*. begun 1758. San Antonio,

LET'S SAY THAT TOGETHER, CLASS. "SPANISH COLONIAL ARCHITECTURE.." VERY GOOD!

SPANISH COLONIAL ARCHITECTURE

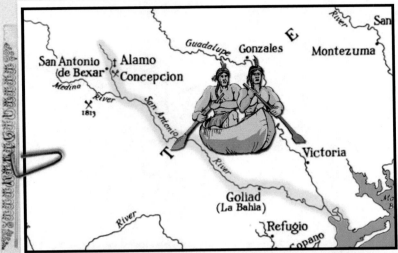

called all of its newly-conquered lands ~~Steve~~ (I mean) New Spain.

The Spanish Empire began building missions in New Spain immediately after Cortez conquered the Aztecs in 1519, and continued to do so for three centuries. Spain established 26 ~~pyramids~~ (I mean) missions in Texas alone. The Alamo is one of the Texan missions.

WHY MISSIONS?

Why did the Spanish construct missions in New Spain? They planned to use the missions to Europeanize their new citizens, the Native Americans. They wanted Native Americans to look, think, and act like ~~football players~~ (I mean) Spaniards.

Despite the fact that the natives already possessed a rich culture of their own, the new Spanish rulers forced Native Americans to abandon their own culture and adopt a ~~new puppy~~ (I mean) a new religion and a new lifestyle. In the

missions, Spanish padres taught them to be Christians as well as farmers, carpenters, and blacksmiths.

COAHUILTECANS AND THE YANAGUANA RIVER

Before the arrival of the Spanish in what we now call Texas, Native Americans, called Coahuiltecans, lived in Texas along the Yanaguana River. In the 1600s Spanish missionaries discovered ~~Pluto~~ (I mean) the Yanaguana River on Saint Anthony de Padua's feast day and renamed it the San Antonio River (see map above).

MISSION SAN ANTONIO DE VALERO

The missionaries then built a mission next to the river and named it Mission San Antonio de Valero after the Christian saint, San Antonio de Padua, and the viceroy of New Spain, the Marquis of Valero.

A PLETHORA OF PROBLEMS

This mission endured a very difficult beginning; it was ~~attacked by alien Elvis impersonators~~ (I mean) destroyed and rebuilt four times over a period of 40 years.

The first mission, built in 1718 on the west side of the San Antonio River, consisted of mud, brush and straw and was built by ~~the three little pigs~~ (I mean) Spanish missionaries.

But this building did not last long. Within a year the padres moved it to the east side of the river to avoid flooding problems. In 1724 a hurricane

54. _Mission San Antonio de Valero (The Alamo)_. begun 1758. San Antonio,

55. _Mission Concepción_. completed 1731. San Antonio, Texas.

destroyed the second mission.

Undaunted, the Spanish erected a third mission in 1744, stronger and larger than the first two. This mission held together until 1750 when a large portion of it spontaneously ~~turned into a giant zucchini~~ (I mean) fell down.

The padres began construction on the final building in 1758, but never finished it. It was this building that General Santa Ana and his men attacked in the Battle of the Alamo.

Later, during the Mexican-American War, the U.S. Army occupied the the mission and made many improvements. They finished the second story and ~~painted it hot pink~~ (I mean) finished the facade of the chapel, giving it its famous rounded top (figure 54).

If it had been finished, historians believe that Mission San Antonio de Valero would look much like the Mission Concepción, also in San Antonio (figure 55). It would have had a bell tower on either side of the entrance and a dome in the back just like the nearby mission.

NOT JUST ONE BUILDING

Most images of the Alamo show only the chapel. But Mission San Antonio de Valero was not just one building. Like most missions, the Alamo was a group of buildings used for living, working, and ~~playing video games~~ (I mean) storing food and other supplies. This is called a mission complex.

The buildings in the mission complex were also connected with thick walls and grouped in a square or rectangle, kind of like a fort, for protection against ~~the big bad wolf~~ (I mean) Apache and Comanche raids.

IF IT'S BAROQUE, DON'T FIX IT

Built in a type of Baroque style, a style fashionable in Europe at the time, the chapel was the most ornate building in the mission complex. Baroque buildings are dramatic, emotional and opulent (very rich-looking). The particular type of Baroque style that the Spanish used in their constructions in New Spain is called Churrigueresque. The padres built Mission

San Antonio de Valero in this style.

WHAT IS CHURRIGUERESQUE?

The Churrigueresque style is similar to the Baroque style but Churrigueresque buildings are also covered with ~~sequins~~ (I mean) intricate sculptural ornaments.

A good example of Churrigueresque architecture is the Cathedral of Santiago de Compostela in Spain. It is dramatic; it grabs your attention. It also arrests your emotions; it fills the viewer with surprise and awe. And it is ~~full of gum balls~~ (I mean) covered with tiny sculptural ornaments or details (figure 56).

In 1828 a French man visited the Alamo and commented that the chapel ~~smelled like a pig pen~~ (I mean) "was overloaded with ornamentation like all the ecclesiastical [religious] buildings of the Spanish colonies." But today the Alamo does not look dramatic or emotional, nor is it full of intricate sculptural ornaments. Why not?

WHAT HAPPENED TO ALL THE FANCY STUFF?

Through the years, wars caused a great amount of damage. But civilians damaged the mission as well. In fact, in 1840 the city of San Antonio sold bricks and other debris from the Alamo for $5 per wagonload! Today the only remaining Churrigueresque ornaments are the four pilasters on either side of the front door (figure 57).

WHAT'S IN A NAME?

Not only was Mission San Antonio de Valero stripped of its ornaments, it was also stripped of its name. In the early 1800s the locals began calling the mission ~~Fred~~ (I mean) the Alamo.

There are two possible sources for the name. A grove of Cottonwood trees stands nearby which in Spanish are called *alamos*. It is possible the name comes from these. Or perhaps the name originated with a group of Spanish soldiers stationed there in 1803 that called themselves the

"~~Flying Opossums~~" (I mean) the "The Alamo Company."

Known originally as the Mission San Antonio de Valero and later as the Alamo, the two names reflect its history as both a mission and ~~a bowling alley~~ (I mean) a fort. But above all, the Alamo is a piece of Spanish Colonial architecture and reflects the needs and desires of the culture that constructed it.

NOW REMEMBER, CLASS, TEXAS IS BIG; ROCKS ARE HEAVY, AND THE ALAMO IS A PIECE OF SPANISH COLONIAL ARCHITECTURE.

56. *Cathedral of Santiago de Compostela* (details). completed 1211 (facade built between 1738-1750). Galicia, Spain.

57. *Mission San Antonio de Valero (The Alamo)*. begun 1758. San Antonio,

1
555

DOO
DADS

Charlie's
Churrigueresque
Choices

WANT YOUR BUILDINGS TO LOOK GNARLY? CALL CHARLIE.

Do your doorways lack detail? Do your pilasters lack pizzazz? Do you suffer from *horror vacui**? Never fear, Charlie is here. Drawing from the eighteenth century style of José Benito de Churriguerra, the inventor of the Churriguerresque style, Charlie and his talented gang will embellish your edifice, bedeck your buildings and festoon your facades.

*the fear of empty spaces

Original

Compare this photograph with the forgery below. Find ten differences. Answers are on page 191.

Forgery

Compare this photograph with the original above. Find ten differences. Answers are on page 191.

AMERICAN ART:
SPANISH COLONIAL ARCHITECTURE
North and South America

BEGAN
1521

ENDED
1821

Monks on a Mission

In which we learn how monks and militiamen conquered the New World for Spain and what mice have to do with it.

THE SPANISH COLONIZE CALIFORNIA

SAN DIEGO, CALIFORNIA, 1769

Today in southern California, Father Junípero Serra and a small band of men arrived in San Diego Bay and, with pomp and circumstance, claimed the spot for Spain.

Since 1492 the Spanish have been as busy as caffeinated beavers subjugating much of the newly-discovered Americas. But unlike the English, who unceremoniously dump boatloads of people on the unsuspecting shores of the New World, the Spanish follow different plans. "We don't send Spaniards **to** the New World, we make Spaniards of the natives **in** the New World." states Goodinn Tenshuns, head of the Sponsor-a-Monk Agency.

"We have a saying: *Conquer, Convert and Coerce.* We *conquer* new land, *convert* the natives to Catholicism and then *coerce* the natives into adopting the Spanish way of life and voila! Spain has new taxpaying citizens."

58. *Mission San Diego de Alcalá*. begun 1774. San Diego, California.

The King of Spain wants to colonize California before Russia does.

MONKS, MISSIONS AND MILITIA MEN

How is this accomplished? "Good question" says Mr. Tenshuns. "We have a another saying: *Monks, Missions and Militia Men.* We send *monks* to the conquered lands, then they build *missions* where they convert and coerce the natives. Where do the *militia men* come in? They protect the monks and the missions. It can get pretty dangerous out there."

"What exactly is a mission? Basically it's a church. But because it is usually the only Spanish outpost for miles around it has to be self-sustaining, therefore each mission includes extra buildings for living quarters, kitchens, workshops, and storerooms. This group of buildings is referred to as a mission complex.

Often in a mission complex all of the rooms are connected in a square or rectangle with a courtyard in the middle. This shape doubles as a fortress. We've already built countless missions throughout the new world" boasts Goodinn.

"So why build more in California? Well, it's just a continuation of what we've been doing in Baja California for years" continued Goodinn. "We already have twenty or so missions down there and San Diego is just the first in what will hopefully be a string of twenty-one missions up the coast of California."

MONKS, MAYHEM AND MICE?

"What's the rush? It's politics" sighs Goodinn Tenshuns. "Rumor has it that the Russians are slowly moving down from the north and the King of Spain

THOSE SURE ARE A LOT OF MISSIONS.

San Francisco de Solano
San Rafael Arcángel
San José
Santa Clara de Asís
Santa Cruz
San Juan Bautista
San Carlos Borromeo de Carmelo
Nuestra Señora de la Soledad
San Antonio de Padua
San Miguel Arcáng
San Luis Obispo de Tolosa
Santa Inés
La Purísima Concepción
Santa Bárbara
San Buenaventura
San Fernando Rey de Espa
San Gabriel Arcángel
San Juan Capistrano
San Luis Rey de Franc
San Diego de Alcalá

wants to claim California before they do. So he's mobilizing monks" concludes Mr. Tenshuns.

"But just because they look like roly-poly bags of potatoes with bald heads, don't underestimate them; monks are a tenacious bunch. We have a saying: *Monks, Mayhem and Mice* . . . wait a minute. That can't be right. Maybe it's *Priests, Persistence and Pandas.* No, no no. How about *Friars, French Fries . . .*"

Burt's Boss Bells

Need to gather your group for grub?
Want to assemble workers for their assignments?

Time to summon worshippers to the sanctuary?

Have to bid mourners to burials?

Buy one of Burt's Boss Bells for all your long-distance communication needs. Gong are the days when any old bell would do. Today smart monks choose Burt's Boss Bells for all their alarming needs. Sound appealing? Chime in with the rest of the clever clergy and say that Burt's Boss Bells are the best bells on the planet.

Buy one of Burt's Boss Bells TODAY!

Original

Compare this photograph with the forgery below. Find ten differences. Answers are on page 191.

Forgery

Compare this photograph with the original above. Find ten differences. Answers are on page 191.

11
The Art of
Benjamin
West

AMERICAN ARTIST:
BENJAMIN WEST
Springfield Township, PA

BORN
October 10, 1738

DIED
March 11, 1820

Benjamin West Modernizes History

TOSSES TOGAS IN THE TRASH

In which we learn about the death of General Wolfe and The Death of General Wolfe, and far too much about dead possums.

PENNSYLVANIA, SOMETIME IN 1770

Recently Mr. Benjamin West, founder of the Royal Academy of Arts in London, unveiled his newest history painting, *The Death of General Wolfe,* to a stunned crowd at the Academy. The room hushed, jaws dropped, and eyes bulged out of their sockets as viewers gazed dumbfoundedly at the latest canvas by this well-respected artist.

"I was flabbergasted." remembers Pahmpus Connisewer, a guest at the event. "No one knew quite what to say. It was brazen, shocking! In this one work Benjamin West broke two of the most important rules for history painting."

RULE NUMBER ONE

The first rule for history painters is this: always paint an ancient event, something that happened hundreds of years ago, not a recent occurrence. West completely disregarded this rule by painting a modern event.

The Death of General Wolfe is an event that occurred at the end of the Battle of

59. West, Benjamin (1738-1820). ***The Death of General Wolfe***. 1770. Oil on canvas, 59 x 84 in. National Gallery of Canada, Ottawa, Canada.

Benjamin West

American artist
10 cents U.S. postage

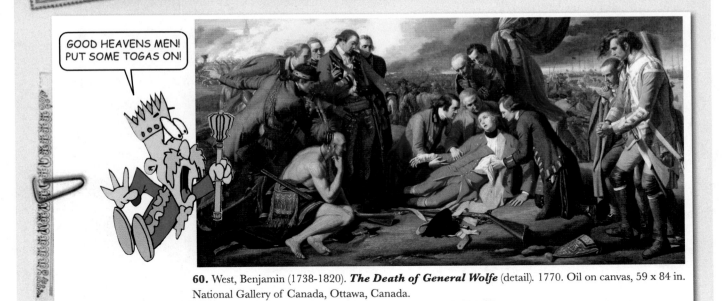

60. West, Benjamin (1738-1820). *The Death of General Wolfe* (detail). 1770. Oil on canvas, 59 x 84 in. National Gallery of Canada, Ottawa, Canada.

Quebec, during the French and Indian war. General Wolfe, a British general, lays dying at the center of the painting just as a messenger brings news that the British have won. General Wolfe is a modern hero not an ancient one.

"Everyone at the unveiling could recall the General's death; it was in all the daily papers. To see it memorialized in oil on a canvas at the Academy was positively scandalous!" states Pahmpus.

"It was disturbing enough to see a recent event on the canvas," continued Mr. Connisewer. "But the second *faux pas* was unforgivable!"

RULE NUMBER TWO

Traditionally in history paintings, all the subjects dress in classical attire; in other words they wear togas. This gives paintings a timeless or ageless quality. Benjamin West chose to ignore that rule and dressed all of the soldiers in contemporary clothing.

"The way he dressed the soldiers was absolutely outrageous! We were shocked! Even the Native American chap is wearing his traditional attire!" exclaims Pahmpus. "Of course King George III didn't approve at all. He begged Ben to put togas on the poor soldiers." But West just couldn't envision the men wrapped in bed sheets with wreaths on their heads. He insisted on modern uniforms.

A GAME CHANGER

"At first we were speechless." remembers Pahmpus. "Then it began to dawn upon us that the effect was no less than brilliant. By dressing the men in modern attire Ben has brought more accuracy to history painting and made it acceptable to paint modern scenes. Mr. West is a genius! I predict that "The Death of General Wolfe" will alter the course of history painting forever."

A General in the Arms is Worth Two in the Bush

AND HE'S NOT PLAYING POSSUM EITHER

IS IT ACCURATE?

"The Death of General Wolfe" is truly a stunning painting, but one can't help asking the question, is it accurate? Was his death really that picturesque? It certainly didn't seem so at the time. When he died, military reports announced that General Wolfe had received a bullet wound to the stomach and died in a ditch near the battlefield surrounded by a few men.

THIS IS GREAT ART

This is not how West depicts it. Ben alters Wolfe's death to represent a more dignified event. In the tradition of great history painting, he wanted to raise the event to a symbolic level.

West does not think it proper for a great general to die under a bush like a wounded possum. He believes he should die as a hero, and heroes do not die under bushes, they die on battlefields surrounded by grieving officers and praying soldiers, with flags flying and ships setting sail in the distance. This is great art; dead possums are not.

COPYING VAN DYCK

As if fabricating the circumstances to magnify his death was not enough, West kicks it up another notch. In his painting General Wolfe expires in the same pose and with the same wound as the crucified Christ in Anthony Van Dyck's sixteenth-century masterpiece, *Deposition* (figures 62 & 63).

THE POSE

In Van Dyck's painting Christ dies in the arms of his mother Mary; in West's painting Wolfe dies in the arms of a fellow officer. By arranging the dying general in the same pose as the

dying Christ, West heightens the symbolism.

THE WOUND

Secondly, both men have been wounded in exactly the same spot. Christ sports a bleeding wound in his side where, while hanging on the cross, a soldier pierced Him with a sword. Likewise Wolfe has been wounded by an enemy bullet in exactly the same place and a soldier covers it with a cloth to stop the flow of blood.

By imitating the pose of Jesus Christ in Van Dyck's masterpiece West upgrades the general's death. Now Wolfe is no longer just a hero dying for his country, but he is a Hero with a capitol "H" sacrificing himself for England just as Christ sacrificed Himself for His church.

By manipulating his death in such a way, no one who looks at this painting smells the stench of the battlefield or senses dead rodents in ditches; they only see combed hair and clean clothes, sacrifice and

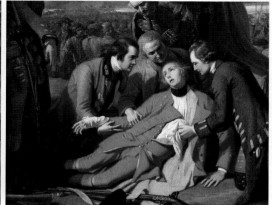

62. Van Dyck, Anthony (1599-1641). ***Deposition***. 1634. Oil on canvas. Alte Pinakothek, Munich, Germany. *This painting is shown in mirror image.*

63. West, Benjamin (1738-1820). ***The Death of General Wolfe***. 1770. Oil on canvas, 59 x 84 in. National Gallery of Canada, Ottawa, Canada.

THE HISTORY PAINTING OF THE YEAR! THE EVENT OF A LIFETIME!

"MR. WEST HAS REINVENTED HISTORY PAINTING!"
-THE NEW YORK WEEKLY

"INNOVATIVE"
- THE FRENCH GAZETTE

THE DEATH OF GENERAL WOLFE

date	location	
1770	**ROYAL ACADEMY OF ARTS**	The phenomenal story of an obscure death raised to the level of a sacrificial hero. Coming soon to a museum near you!

Original

Compare this painting with the forgery below. Find ten differences.
Answers are on page 192.

Forgery

Compare this painting with the original above. Find ten differences.
Answers are on page 192.

AMERICAN ARTIST:
BENJAMIN WEST
Philadelphia, PA

BORN
October 10, 1738

DIED
March 11, 1820

Ben and Penn Remember When

TREAT YOUR EYES TO A PICTURE OF PENN'S TREATY

In which we investigate the symbolism of *William Penn's Treaty with the Indians,* and endure a plethora of really bad puns.

PHILADELPHIA, SOMETIME IN 1772

Eighty-nine years ago William Penn and Tamanend, a Lenape chief, met under a large, shady elm tree in a Lenape village called Shackamaxon, in what we now call Pennsylvania. Here, in 1682, they approved an historic peace treaty. Recently Mr. Thomas Penn, son of the late William Penn, commissioned Benjamin West to memorialize this event in oil. We here at the *Pennsylvania Press* interviewed Mr. Penn about this painting.

US: So, what's this painting about, besides the obvious.

THOMAS: It's about peace. "Pop was all about peace." comments his son. "I think Ben captured the mood perfectly in the painting. It's very tranquil and harmonious. No one is shooting anyone else or poking anyone in the ribs or making bunny ears

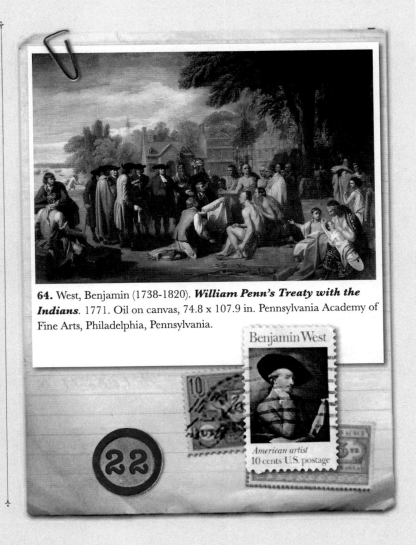

64. West, Benjamin (1738-1820). ***William Penn's Treaty with the Indians***. 1771. Oil on canvas, 74.8 x 107.9 in. Pennsylvania Academy of Fine Arts, Philadelphia, Pennsylvania.

Benjamin West

American artist
10 cents U.S. postage

22

65-67. West, Benjamin (1738-1820). ***William Penn's Treaty with the Indians*** (detail). 1771. Oil on canvas, 74.8 x 107.9 in. Pennsylvania Academy of Fine Arts, Philadelphia, Pennsylvania.

behind their head. It's just men doing business. The dock workers at the far left of the painting are taking a break from their sweating and swearing to watch the peaceful event. The baby isn't even crying. And notice how the native seated at the center of the canvas, one of Tamanend's men, lays aside his bow and arrows (a symbol of war) and grasps a peace pipe (a symbol of peace). Perfect symbolism. Dad would be pleased.

US: Is that your father standing there with his arms wide open looking like the man on the oatmeal box?

THOMAS: Yep, that's him. Don't tell Ben, but he looks too old and paunchy in the painting. He was quite young and twiggy in 1682. In fact he used to challenge the natives to races and sometime even won! Can't do that looking like a lard bucket. Ben must have used a much later portrait to copy from.

US: Dad was a bit of a butterball in his later years?

THOMAS: Let's just say he lived large.

US: Is there anything else that isn't quite right?

THOMAS: Well, no one built houses like that in 1682, and the river wasn't as crowded. That part of the painting looks more like a photograph from today rather than from a century ago.

US: What's a photograph?

THOMAS: No idea.

US: Okay. Let's talk about the composition. Compare this painting to West's famous work, *The Death of General Wolfe.*

THOMAS: Well, in both paintings the people are divided into three groups. In *The Death of General Wolfe* there are three groups of soldiers: one group on the left dramatically agonizing over the dying general and one group on the right dramatically agonizing over the dying general, and a third group in the middle . . .

US: Let me guess: dramatically agonizing over the dying general?

The diagonal lines in *The Death of General Wolfe* represent the turmoil and instability of war.

THE STABLE LINES IN THE *TREATY WITH THE INDIANS* SYMBOLIZE PEACE.

THOMAS: Nope, they are dramatically *holding* the dying general.

In *William Penn's Treaty with the Indians* there are also three groups of people: in the center group the Quakers and the Natives attentively watch the business transaction. Then there are the dock workers on the left who are attentively watching the business transaction, and the group of natives on the right who . . .

US: Attentively watch the business transaction?

THOMAS: No, actually they seem to be totally ignoring them, except maybe the little girl (figure 67).

US: Fascinating. What else?

THOMAS: The composition (the way people and things are arranged in the painting) of *The Death of General Wolfe* consists of diagonal lines to represent the turmoil and instability of war; many of the soldiers lean toward General Wolfe, and the flag draws the eye to the center of the canvas (figure 68).

In contrast, in *William Penn's Treaty with the Indians* Ben uses stable vertical lines to represent the security and strength of peace. The houses, the men, the trunk of the great elm all stand straight, firm and immobile as they work out the treaty (figure 69).

US: Fascinating. Hey, maybe that's why Mr. West made your father so portly. Perhaps he thought it added, um, "weight" to the composition.

THOMAS: Fat chance.

US: I'm just trying to plump up the conversation.

THOMAS: Thanks a ton.

US: I guess that was laying it on a bit thick.

THOMAS: By and large.

US: Well, it is with a heavy heart that we end this interview and say good-bye. Thanks for taking time to talk to us today; it was real big of you.

THOMAS: It's a load off my mind.

68. West, Benjamin (1738-1820). *The Death of General Wolfe*. 1770. Oil on canvas, 59 x 84 in. National Gallery of Canada, Ottawa, Canada.

69. West, Benjamin (1738-1820). *William Penn's Treaty with the Indians*. 1771. Oil on canvas, 74.8 x 107.9 in. Pennsylvania Academy of Fine Arts, Philadelphia, Pennsylvania.

VISIT

PENN TREATY PARK

In the old Lenape Village of Shackamaxon

Near the heart of downtown Philadelphia

Want to picnic where Penn and Tamanend proposed peace?

Want to promenade your pooch by the scenic Delaware River?

Feeling nostalgic? Come to picturesque Penn Treaty Park. With a large grassy lawn and a tall statue of Penn where the giant elm once stood, Penn Treaty Park marks the spot where William Penn and Chief Tamanend sealed a treaty that promised peace between the Lenape tribes and the Europeans. What better way to remember the love and friendship that two groups of people can have than by breaking out the baloney and cheese, and throwing tennis balls for your dog.
Penn Treaty Park: THE GLEN WHERE PENN MET WITH SOME MEN.

Original

Compare this painting with the forgery below. Find ten differences.
Answers are on page 192.

Forgery

Compare this painting with the original above. Find ten differences.
Answers are on page 192.

12

The Art of
John Singleton
Copley

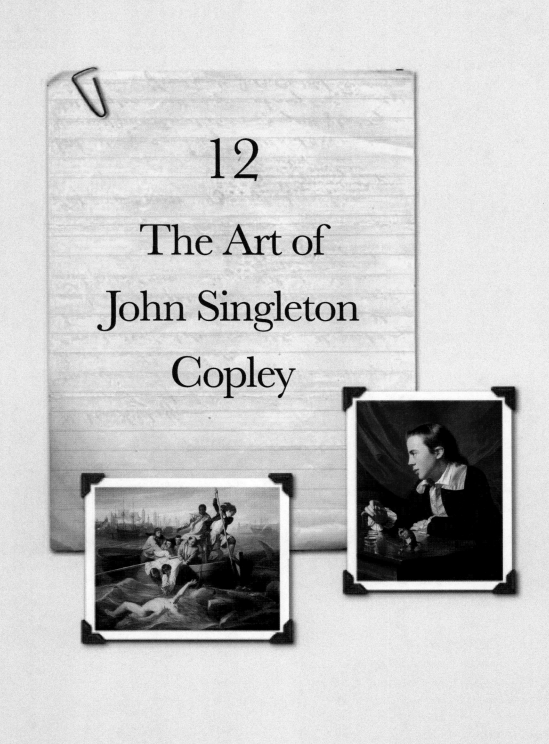

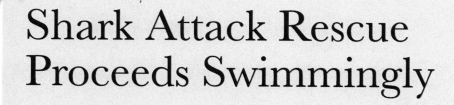

AMERICAN ARTIST:
JOHN SINGLETON COPLEY
Boston, MA

BORN
1738

DIED
September 9, 1815

In which we learn that sharks have sharp teeth, no lips, and why swimming naked in the bay is a bad idea.

Shark Attack Rescue Proceeds Swimmingly

TRUE STORY MEMORIALIZED IN OIL 29 YEARS LATER

BOSTON, SOMETIME IN 1778

On a bright warm day in Havana Bay in 1749, fourteen-year-old Brook Watson, crew member on a trading ship, decided to take advantage of the good weather and take a swim in the bay in the buff, as was the custom of the times.

ONE FOOT IN THE GRAVE

"The shark came out of no where." says Mr. Watson, now 43 and a prosperous merchant in London. "It circled me a couple of times then took a chunk of flesh off my lower right leg. Blood coursed into the water as the beast returned. On his second pass he devoured my right foot. Just before he finished me off help arrived."

NEVER A DULL MOMENT

It is this moment that John Singleton Copley captures in his stunning oil painting *Watson and the Shark*. In the background the viewer recognizes a serene Havana harbor, but the foreground boils with anxiety and suspense, as nine men from Brook's vessel pull together in a rescue effort.

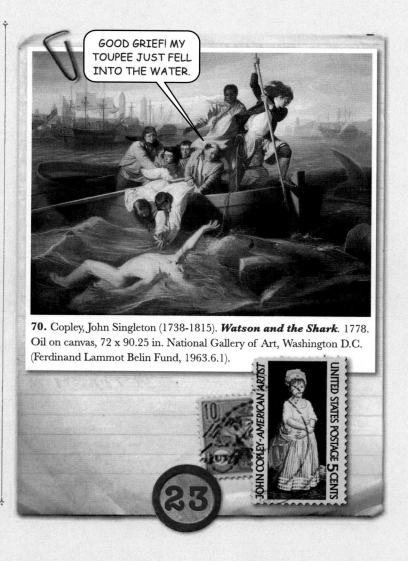

70. Copley, John Singleton (1738-1815). *Watson and the Shark*. 1778. Oil on canvas, 72 x 90.25 in. National Gallery of Art, Washington D.C. (Ferdinand Lammot Belin Fund, 1963.6.1).

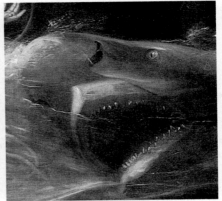

71-72. Copley, John Singleton (1738-1815). *Watson and the Shark* (detail). 1778. Oil on canvas, 72 x 90.25 in. National Gallery of Art, Washington D.C. (Ferdinand Lammot Belin Fund, 1963.6.1).

RUB-A-DUB-DUB, NINE MEN IN A TUB

Sitting in the dingy four men strain at the oars, racing the shark to reach Mr. Watson in time. Two sailors reach over the edge in an attempt to capture the swimmer with their hands while a third keeps them from falling in. Standing above in the back, another friend tosses a rope to Brook that drapes over his outstretched arm (figure 71). Finally a brave mariner raises a spear on the verge of plunging it into the pursuing animal.

"I remember my pals screaming and the searing pain in my leg," recalls Brook. "I never felt the rope on my arm or saw the outstretched hands. I was in shock."

A CRITIC'S APPRAISAL

The *Boston Bait* turns to a professional for comment. "It's a phenomenal piece of art painted in the latest style," gushes Ayemen Awhe, art critic for the London Royal Academy of Arts in London, where the painting debuted to a fawning crowd. "Mr. Copley has captured the action at its peak without giving away the outcome. He perfectly imparts to the viewer the angst of the moment."

LIVING, FOR THE MOMENT

"I, for one, could have done with a little less angst," retorts Watson. "Not knowing if I still had a foot, not knowing if my friends could reach me in time, not knowing where the shark was, the angst was just a little too much. However, if Copley was looking for a moment in which the tension was at its peak, that was definitely it."

THE UNSUNG HEROES

"John Copley is following in the avant-garde footsteps of Benjamin West," Ayemen continues. "He has taken an everyday experience and raised it to heroic levels which, until West, were reserved only for events in the distant past. Before West, most historical paintings depicted things like victories in battle, a moment of surrender, the death of a god, things like that. But a painting of a shark consuming a boy's foot for lunch? That's definitely a departure from the norm."

"According to Copley, heroic deeds do not have to involve armies or gods," Mr. Awe continues. "A group of friends risking their lives to rescue their buddy from the scaly jaws of death can be just as moving. Under Mr. Copley's well-disciplined brush, this humble event of local courage becomes a symbol of salvation at the highest levels."

SHARKS DON'T HAVE LIPS

On a purely practical level, however, it's pretty obvious that Mr. Copley never actually saw a real shark," Ayemen adds. "If he had, he would know that real sharks don't have lips (figure 72)."

Original

Compare this painting with the forgery
below. Find ten differences.
Answers are on page 192.

Forgery

Compare this painting with the original
above. Find ten differences.
Answers are on page 192.

JOHN SINGLETON COPLEY
PORTRAIT ARTIST

Tired of waiting for the camera to be invented? Need to immortalize Great Aunt Mabel before she kicks the bucket? Want a painting of your shiny gold, smooth silks, lustrous glass, and fabulous furs to show off your wealth?

Then look to John Singleton Copley to paint it all! Mr. Copley painted this portrait of his younger step-brother, Henry Pelham (and his pet squirrel, Mike), to show off his ability to paint a variety of substances, surfaces and textures.

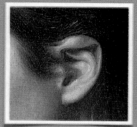

If you fancy satin, the red curtain behind Henry shows that John can paint the fanciest satin this side of the pond.

Mike's fuzzy little tuckus displays John's ability to forge faux fur.

In addition, Mike's delicate gold leash demonstrates John's ability to render precious metals.

Convincing expressions are John's specialty. Henry's dreamy display is so lifelike he could be watching the latest Batman cartoon.

Want a clear crystal glass of crystal clear liquid included in your portrait? John's your man!

Sumptuous silk simply slides off John's brush. Henry's pink collar shows slick skill in simulating silk. (His mother made him wear it).

Want to make your viewers swoon with envy? (Yes, swoon!) John will paint wood that shines so realistically you'll really take a shine to it.

Finally, John can paint crushed velvet that will make your mouth water, if you like eating crushed velvet, that is.

Big-time British artist Joshua Reynolds has already seen this portrait of Henry and is encouraging Copley to come to England to pursue his painting career. So hire John today . . . before it's too late!

Forgery

Compare this painting with the original
on the left. Find ten differences.
Answers are on page 192.

Original

Compare this painting with the forgery
on the right. Find ten differences.
Answers are on page 192.

13
The Art of
Paul Revere

AMERICAN ARTIST:
PAUL REVERE
Boston, MA

BORN
January 1, 1735

DIED
May 10, 1818

In which we learn what organic design is and that hot metal looks the same as cold metal.

Paul Revere Goes for Baroque!

MAKES SILVER IN BAROQUE AND ROCOCO STYLES

BOSTON, SOMETIME IN 1775

Today, we here at *The Boston Brain* are interviewing Mr. Ahrt Eckspurt, art critic for the *London Times,* about one of our beloved local silversmiths, Mr. Paul Revere.

US: So, Mr. Eckspurt, tell us about Paul.

AHRT: Well, Paul is a splendid artisan who's silver pieces demonstrate many aspects of the Baroque (*pronounced buh-ROKE)* and Rococo art movement.

US: Whoa dude, slow down. Most of our readership shines their shoes with their saliva. Explain. What are the Baroque and Rococo art movements?

AHRT: The Baroque movement began in the 1600s in Italy and has since spread throughout Europe. It is a style of art that is dramatic and full of details and motion. Rococo is a style that grew out of the Baroque, and is a little more free flowing, more ornate and generally more fun.

US: Okay, so how does Paul's work demonstrate this dramatic, free flowing, ornate art?

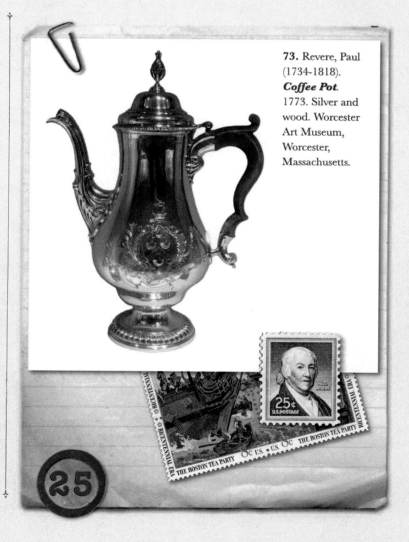

73. Revere, Paul (1734-1818). *Coffee Pot.* 1773. Silver and wood. Worcester Art Museum, Worcester, Massachusetts.

That's what hot right now in the colonies: European stuff.

THAT'S WHY PAUL COPIES THE BAROQUE AND ROCOCO STYLES

AHRT: Well, for example, his pieces are rhythmic and curvy; this makes the artworks look like they are moving or flowing.

US: Like the spout and the handle on the coffee pot (figure 73)?

AHRT: Exactly.

US: Tell us more.

AHRT: They are asymmetrical. In other words, they are uneven or not uniform.

US: Anything else?

AHRT: The decoration or engraving on the coffee pot is organic.

US: Wait. You mean it was grown without pesticides or synthetic fertilizers? I don't get it.

AHRT: Uh, not exactly. In this instance organic means natural, as in the opposite of geometric. Organic designs imitate nature. They look like leaves and flowers, not triangles and diamonds (figure 74-75).

US: Ah. That kind of organic. Speaking of organic, why is the teapot handle made of wood and not silver?

AHRT: The handle is made of wood for practical reasons: wood doesn't conduct heat and therefore remains cool to the touch when the vessel is filled with hot coffee.

US: Ah, the old "hot metal looks the same as cold metal, but wood is never hot unless it's on fire" saying.

AHRT: Huh?

US: Never mind. What's with the pineapple on the top of the coffee pot? Was that Paul's favorite fruit (figure 76)?

AHRT: Nope, the pineapple design is a recent Rococo development and demonstrates that Paul is at the cutting edge of his business.

US: Why does Paul bother with the Baroque and Rococo styles? Why doesn't he just make up a new Colonial style or something?

AHRT: Good question. Now let me ask you one.

US: Shoot.

AHRT: Why does Paul work as a silversmith?

US: Easy. To support his eleven children.

74-76. Revere, Paul (1734-1818). ***Coffee Pot*** (details). 1773. Silver and wood. Worcester Art Museum, Worcester, Massachusetts.

77. Halsall, William. *Mayflower in Plymouth Harbor.* 1882. Oil painting. Pilgrim Hall Museum, Plymouth, MA.

AHRT: Right. In other words, to make a living. And in order to make a living he needs to make things that his clients want to buy, things that reflect the tastes of his patrons. What do his patrons want?

US: Hot dogs, french fries and apple pie?

AHRT: Nope. His patrons want what's trendy in Europe. That's what's hot right now in the colonies: European stuff. That's why Paul copies the Baroque and Rococo styles.

US: I see.

AHRT: What does all this mean in the grand scheme of things, you might ask?

US: We might, but we didn't.

AHRT: Well, I'm going to answer anyway. It's important.

US: Knock yourself out.

AHRT: The fact that Mr. Revere is using new European styles for his art here in the colonies means that European culture is making the trip across the pond.

US: Why is that important?

AHRT: It's evidence, my friend, evidence that America is stepping up in the world, that you're not isolated. You're no longer just a bunch of colonial yokels trying to eek out a living on this rock you call America. You're actually accumulating time and money to spend on taste and culture. It's important because it means that America is now part of the larger European scene; you're not isolated. You're becoming players in the international game of parcheesi, so to speak.

US: You mean some day we might even use shoe polish?

AHRT: We can only hope.

Paul Revere's
Shiny Silver Shop

For all your fine silver needs.
Remember, everything that glitters isn't gold.

HMM . . . I THINK I LIKE SHINY THINGS.

Has America been good to you?

Extra cash burning a hole in your pocket?

Are you climbing the colonial social ladder? Got a hankering to add a little refinement to your residence, some dignity to your domicile, panache to your pad? Come to Paul Revere's Shiny Silver Shop! If you're looking for the appearance of affluence, Paul's your man! He can create all the trappings of an aristocratic lifestyle for your dining room table. Paul's silver pieces aren't just functional, they're works of art modeled in the latest Baroque and Rococo designs. Want something shiny? Then rush your hiney to our showroom today!

Forgery

Compare this piece of silver with the original on the left. Find ten differences. Answers are on page 192.

Original

Compare this piece of silver with the forgery on the right. Find ten differences. Answers are on page 192.

AMERICAN ARTIST:
PAUL REVERE
Boston, MA

BORN
January 1, 1735

DIED
May 10, 1818

In which we learn about the Boston Massacre and why ballerinas never wear black boots.

Paul Bends the Truth and Breaks the News

SKEWS PUBLIC OPINION TOWARD REBELLION

BOSTON, 1770

Bostonians are lining up in droves to purchase Paul Revere's latest print, *The Bloody Massacre,* in which Paul points a finger at the British redcoats for the killing of five Bostonians. It's been only twenty-one days since the actual event and Paul's dramatic portrayal of the tragedy is selling like hotcakes. But is it news or is it propaganda?

PROBABLY PROPAGANDA

"Definitely propaganda." declares Onthespaht Reeportuhr, star journalist for *The Boston Brain.* "Paul's account is wrong. He's exaggerating the event for political reasons. That's just not the way it happened."

"First, the British didn't organize an attack. Paul shows the British lining up like ballerinas and firing at the command of a general as if this were a prearranged engagement in a war (figure 78). That's not what happened. No one planned this. It was a spontaneous riot. Sure, someone yelled "fire" Onthespaht admits, "but no on knows who. Only a couple of soldiers shot randomly into the mob, yet Revere

FORGET YOUR TOES, MEN, THIS IS A BATTLE, NOT A BALLET!

78. Revere, Paul (1734-1818). ***The Bloody Massacre.*** 1770. Engraving with watercolor, 25.8 x 33.4 cm. (plate). Library of Congress, Washington D.C.

26

79-80. Revere, Paul (1734-1818). *The Bloody Massacre* (details). 1770. Engraving with watercolor, 25.8 x 33.4 cm. (plate). Library of Congress, Washington D.C.

displays the whole detachment firing in concert."

BAD BLOOD

"I'll agree with Paul that the incident was brutal" concedes Onthespaht. "Five Bostonians died and four more sustained serious injuries. Paul would call them innocent bystanders, but I wouldn't. Sure, the Bostonians were bystanders, but they were definitely not innocent."

"In Paul's version of the event the colonials lie empty-handed, unarmed, oozing patriot blood, consoling each other, and dying as martyrs on the cold, icy pavement. The whole scene could have been stolen from a bad soap opera. But the truth is, the patriots provoked the attack. Prior to the shots, bitter and enraged Bostonians threw ice and snow, as well as insults, at a British sentry who called to his buddies for aid."

"But the most obvious exaggeration in the image is the sign above the Royal Custom's House" continues Onthespaht. "Because the British occupy this office in Boston, Paul labels it 'Butcher's Hall' (figure 80) to encourage the viewers to see the redcoats as cleaver-waving savages slaughtering angelic townspeople. Again, this is far from the truth."

A DOG AND PONY SHOW

"Finally, the dog at the bottom is a syrupy touch," adds Onthespaht (figure 79). "And it's not just because the pup is so cute and cuddly. Notice that it is standing on the colonists' side of the print. That's so the viewer will identify the Bostonians with the dog's innocence and faithfulness. And those qualities glaringly contrast with the "brutality" of the British. It's as if the poor shivering Bostonians were just standing around looking cute when all of a

sudden the British lined up and fired uopn them."

"This is really going to skew public opinion." states Mr. Reeportuhr. "And I'm sure that is what Paul is hoping for. The British soldiers who fired the shots are on trial and already the judge has had to warn the jurors not to be influenced by Paul's print."

BLOOD ON HIS HANDS

"There is no doubt that this image is going to intensify demand for a full-scale rebellion," laments Mr. Reeportuhr. "I sure hope Paul knows what he is doing."

W A N T E D

PAUL REVERE: Suspected of Plagiarism

Pelham's Printing Press suspects Paul Revere of plagiarism and hopes to prosecute. Although people praise Paul for propping up patriotism and printing propaganda, his prestige may be polluted. Henry Pelham, printer and step-brother to prominent painter John Singleton Copley, proposes that Paul pilfered the portrayal of the protest from his picture (which is more proficient and precise than Paul's). Paul impertinently peddled his print so promptly that by the time Pelham put his picture to press, passion for the protest was all pooped out. No one would purchase Pelham's product. Paul has never professed to the pernicious performance and Pelham is out a pile of pesos.

Pelham's Printing Press: proudly providing premium products at competitive prices.

Forgery

Compare this print with the original on the left. Find ten differences. Answers are on page 193.

Original

Compare this print with the forgery on the right. Find ten differences. Answers are on page 193.

14

The Art of
Charles
Willson Peale

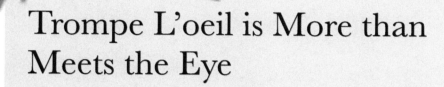

AMERICAN ARTIST:
CHARLES WILLSON PEALE
Chester, MD

BORN
April 15, 1741

DIED
February 22, 1827

Trompe L'oeil is More than Meets the Eye

In which we learn about trompe l'oeil, and allegories. We also find out that Charles Willson Peale was a crafty old coot.

IT RHYMES WITH "STOMP THE TOY"

PHILADELPHIA, 1795

What is a *trompe l'oeil* you ask? Technically it's French for "deceive the eye." In practice, it is a trick, a hoax, an illusion, a fake. In short, a *trompe l'oeil* is a painting that wants you to think it's reality.

Charles Willson Peale''s *Staircase Group* (figure 81) is a *trompe l'oeil*. In this full-length double portrait, Peale's sons, Raphaelle and Titian, stand on a *faux* (fake) staircase and look back at the viewer slyly, as if to say "I dare you to follow me." *Trompe l'oeil* is sneaky business.

HOW DOES IT WORK?

How does Peale's *Staircase Group* "deceive the eye?" Let's begin with the two young men. First, they're life-sized. Though obvious, this is extremely important since a smaller portrait would hardly be deceptive. Who would be tempted to follow two miniature young men up a doll-sized staircase?

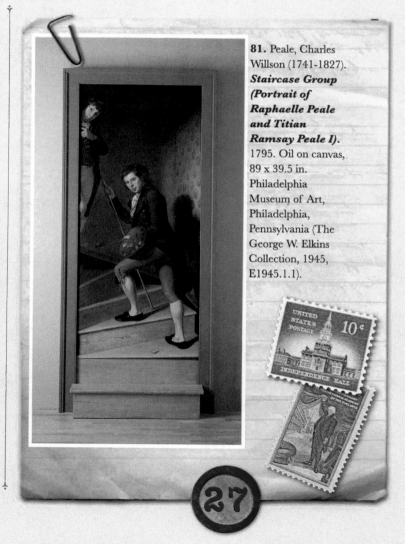

81. Peale, Charles Willson (1741-1827). ***Staircase Group (Portrait of Raphaelle Peale and Titian Ramsay Peale I).*** 1795. Oil on canvas, 89 x 39.5 in. Philadelphia Museum of Art, Philadelphia, Pennsylvania (The George W. Elkins Collection, 1945, E1945.1.1).

27

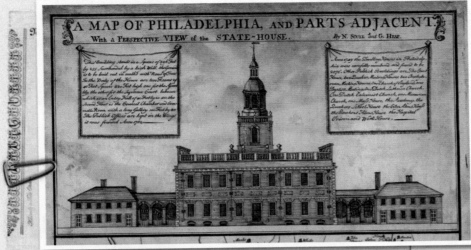

A MAP OF PHILADELPHIA, AND PARTS ADJACENT.
With a PERSPECTIVE VIEW of the STATE-HOUSE. By N. SCULL and G. HEAP.

82. Scull, N. and Heap, G. *A Map of Philadelphia and Parts Adjacent.* (detail of north elevation of Independence Hall). 1752. Map, American Memory Collections, Library of Congress's Geography & Map Division, Washington D.C.

THEY'VE BEEN FRAMED

Secondly, the frame adds to the illusion. If you visit the Columbianum this Friday, you will see the painting in its intended surroundings. You will find that the *Staircase Group* is not mounted in a normal frame. No ornate gold chichi frame for this painting. Chuck framed this baby with something rather unusual: a real doorway.

Peale designed this canvas to stand in a closet doorway in the assembly room of Independence Hall. The moulding around the doorway substitutes as the picture frame so that when the painting is in place, it appears to the viewer as though the doorway opens into a staircase with two young men standing on it.

WATCH YOUR STEP

To increase the deception, Peale added a real wooden step at the bottom of the painted steps. We here at the *Pennsylvania Poppycock* are betting that, when the exhibition opens, many people will try to climb this step and smack their noses into the canvas.

(We're bringing popcorn and peanuts for the show.)

IN A GOOD LIGHT

Lighting in the painting is also important. In the assembly room the sun pours in from the south, therefore since the *Staircase Group* hangs on the west wall, the shadows in the painting should fall to the right. Ol' Chuck didn't miss this detail; the shadows in the painting bend to the right, mimicking the shadows cast by the real step and closet door frame.

EXCUSE ME, YOU DROPPED SOMETHING

The trickery continues. Check out the tiny scrap of paper lying on the bottom step (figure 84). Did Raphaelle drop something? Is it a note, a list, a love letter from his girlfriend, a receipt from the local Piggly-Wiggly? None of the above. It is an admission

Peale created the Columbianum to encourage the colonists to pursue the arts.

HE WANTS THEM TO LEARN HOW TO THINK ABOUT ART AND HOW TO DO ART.

ticket to the Peale Museum. Instead of signing this painting, Mr. Peale embedded his identity on this tiny piece of paper. He slipped this in as a clever way of claiming authorship of the painting and as a sly advertisement for his family's science institution.

THE MUSEUM IS THAT WAY

The Peale Museum is just down the street. So grab your fake ticket and head on down. In case you don't know where it is, *faux* Titian will show you.

In the portrait Titian is slyly pointing toward his right (figure 83). If the viewer looks in that direction, he will look out the windows on the south wall of the assembly room and see Philosophical Hall, the building next door, which houses

said museum. Peale is a shameless, crafty old coot, isn't he.

THEORY AND PRACTICE

He's crafty and he's subtle. Peale created the Columbianum to encourage the colonists to pursue the theory and practice of the fine arts. In other words, he wanted the colonists to learn both how to *think* about art and how to *do* art.

Peale subtly encoded the Columbianum's mission into the *Staircase Group*. How does Peale embed this in the painting? Titian and Raphaelle represent the traditional allegories of Theory and Practice.

WHAT IS AN ALLEGORY?

An allegory is a symbolic figure that stands for an idea. The first allegory

that Charles represents in his painting is Practice. Traditionally artists represented Practice as a woman holding tools and climbing a staircase. The staircase represents gradual upward improvement which is, of course, the result of diligent *practice*.

What about Theory? The allegory of Theory is commonly represented descending a staircase holding nothing, because she is, well, thinking deeply about her theories.

In the *Staircase Group*, Raphaelle and Titian represent the allegories of Theory and Practice. Raphaelle, the older boy, holds a palette and a maul stick, tools of the artist's trade. He ascends the stairs symbolizing the improvement that Practice brings. Titian, the younger boy,

83-84. Peale, Charles Willson (1741-1827). ***Staircase Group (Portrait of Raphaelle Peale and Titian Ramsay Peale I)*** (details). 1795. Oil on canvas, 89 x 39.5 in. Philadelphia Museum of Art, Philadelphia, Pennsylvania (The George W. Elkins Collection, 1945, E1945.1.1).

The Columbianum is both an art exhibition and a new art school.

PEALE WANTS TO EDUCATE NEW ARTISTS AND THE PUBLIC ABOUT ART.

descends the staircase holds nothing but the thoughts in his head, representing the allegory of Theory.

THE IMPORTANCE OF EDUCATION

In the *Staircase Group* Mr. Peale summoned all of his skills of illusion and trickery. His purpose? To demonstrate his talent, of course, but also to emphasize the importance of art education.

Peale is all about art education. (Every one of his 17 children is learning to paint.) Not only are Theory and Practice trying to trick you into following them up the stairs, they are also trying to entice you to follow them in their pursuit of the arts.

Which leads us back to the Columbianum. The Columbianum is not only an art exhibition, but a new art school that Peale has dreamed about for years. Chuck is hoping that the new art institution will not only help train a new generation of artists, but also educate the general public in art appreciation.

IT EVEN FOOLED GEORGE

So not only does the double portrait of Raphaelle and Titian have some serious prank potential (rumor has it that even the famous George Washington tipped his hat to the young men on the stairs the other day), but on a more serious note, the portrait also represents Charles Willson Peale's hopes and dreams for future art education in the Colonies, and for his new fine arts academy.

85. Peale, Charles Willson (1741-1827). ***Staircase Group (Portrait of Raphaelle Peale and Titian Ramsay Peale I)*** (detail). 1795. Oil on canvas, 89 x 39.5 in. Philadelphia Museum of Art, Philadelphia, Pennsylvania (The George W. Elkins Collection, 1945, E1945.1.1).

CHARLES WILLSON PEALE'S COLUMBIANUM

America's first art exhibition launches America's first art academy.

The presentation begins Friday night in the Assembly Room at Independence Hall at 8:00pm. Charles Willson Peale and associates invites one and all to attend the the unprecedented art premier of the century: the Columbianum. This is both the title of the exhibition and the name of the new academy. Confusing? You bet! Way to go Chuck.

The Columbianum will display artworks galore: portraits, landscapes, even model ships! There will be over 150 total entries. This exhibition brings together such famous artists as Benjamin West, John Singleton Copley, Charles Willson Peale, James Peale, Raphaelle Peale, Rembrandt Peale, Orange Peale, Apple Peale . . . just kidding!

The Columbianum couldn't be at a more distinguished location. The Pennsylvania State House has a glorious history: within its walls America declared her independence and behind its doors the founders wrote the Constitution. The State House also hosted the first and second Continental Congresses. You won't find a more celebrated place in the entire country! (You won't find any bigger rooms either.)

The new art academy, the Columbianum will not only serve artists, but also will strive to educate the public in the fine arts. Peale's all about education for the local yokels. So put on your Sunday best and go soak up some culture, you clodhopper!

Original

Compare this painting with the forgery
on the right. Find ten differences.
Answers are on page 191.

Forgery

Compare this painting with the original
on the left. Find ten differences.
Answers are on page 191.

AMERICAN ARTIST:
CHARLES WILLSON PEALE
Chester, MD

BORN
April 15, 1741

DIED
February 22, 1827

In which we discuss battles, cannon, Hessians, and Uncle George who pulls coins out of his ears at birthday parties.

Pennsylvania "Big Guns" Order Portrait of a "Big Gun"

PEALE'S PRINCETON PORTRAIT IS APPEALING

PHILADELPHIA, SOMETIME IN 1779

On Tuesday of this week Charles Willson Peale, London-trained painter and mammoth bone collector, delivered a full-length portrait of General George Washington to the Supreme Executive Council of Pennsylvania (SEC) here in Philadelphia. Established just two years ago, the SEC is the highest governing body in Pennsylvania. They're the big wigs, the top brass, the big guns, the stuffed shirts, the suits (always black or blue), and after viewing the portrait for the first time, they're tickled pink.

"It's just what we wanted" sighed Bohring Loyour IV. "In this painting Washington is victorious and heroic, majestic yet familiar. Peale's work is a symbol of strength and freedom and embodies all of our aspirations for these colonies."

Charles Willson Peale has painted George Washington more times than any other painter. He also painted the earliest portrait of him in 1772, the only likeness

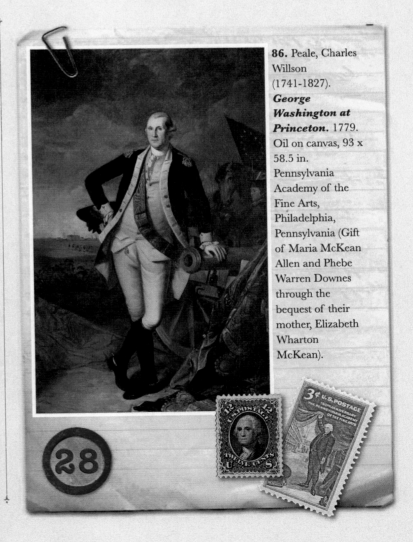

86. Peale, Charles Willson (1741-1827). *George Washington at Princeton.* 1779. Oil on canvas, 93 x 58.5 in. Pennsylvania Academy of the Fine Arts, Philadelphia, Pennsylvania (Gift of Maria McKean Allen and Phebe Warren Downes through the bequest of their mother, Elizabeth Wharton McKean).

87. Peale, Charles Willson (1741-1827). *George Washington at Princeton* (detail). 1779. Oil on canvas, 93 x 58.5 in. Pennsylvania Academy of the Fine Arts, Philadelphia, Pennsylvania (Gift of Maria McKean Allen and Phebe Warren Downes through the bequest of their mother, Elizabeth Wharton McKean).

of the General completed before the Revolutionary War.

In *George Washington at Princeton* (figure 86), Washington stands victorious at the scene of the Battle of Princeton in New Jersey. Considered one of George's greatest victories, the colonists fought the Battle of Princeton directly after another famous battle, the Battle of Trenton, in which George and his troops made their famous nighttime crossing of the treacherous and icy Delaware River. Together, both of these battles represented a turning point for morale in the Revolutionary War.

To identify the battle, Peale places Nassau Hall, the main building on Princeton University's campus, in the background (figure 87). He also included this building in the painting because they fought the end of the Battle of Princeton inside Nassau Hall. Yes, *inside* the building!

Outside the hall, soldiers take sixteen redcoats prisoner and march them off across the field (figure 87). The victory is an exhilarating moment for the Colonial army.

At the center of the canvas, standing tall and proud, and slightly gangly, and maybe a teeny bit paunchy, is the hero and subject of the painting: General George Washington. A blue sash strapped across his chest identifies him as the Commander-in-Chief. (It also brings out the color of his eyes.) His gangliness and paunchiness are not a mistake, it is reality. Peale painted George as he really appeared. This portrait is one of the most authentic portraits of Washington ever painted.

Of course he wears more than just a blue sash; he is decked out in full military regalia: gold tassel thingies on his shoulders, polished boots, brass buttons, starched cuffs and fluffy ruffles (say that five times in a hurry).

Neither is he alone. An officer stands behind him with his noble mare at the ready. All these details emphasize Washington's importance

Being a hero requires more than just looking cool; it requires action.

THE CANNON DENOTES DETERMINATION, BRAVERY, MOXIE AND GRIT.

and distinction. He is a war hero, a general, a leader.

But being a hero requires more than just looking cool; it requires action. Ol' George is an active guy and this painting is full of symbols of his gutsy activities. The most prominent and obvious one is the captured cannon that he leans upon. It's presence in the painting denotes determination, bravery, moxie and grit, *true grit*. John Wayne would have been proud.

That stuff at his feet isn't his dirty laundry, it's the flags of troops he and his men defeated. By his right foot lies the British flag from the Battle at Princeton and on the

ground at his left are two Hessian flags that Washington's guys captured at the Battle of Trenton. (The Hessians are those hefty, intimidating German soldier dudes that the British hired to fight the colonists.)

But there is more. In Peale's portrait George is more than heroic, he is also majestic, aristocratic. While in London, Peale examined a variety of formal portraits of royalty, nobles, dukes and other blue-blooded folks. Among them he viewed the *Portrait of Augustus John, Third Earl of Bristol* (figure 88) by Thomas Gainsborough who strikes a similar pose

as does Washington on this canvas. But unlike Gainsborough's gentlemen, Washington is unpretentious, humble, modest, laid-back, maybe even folksy. He does not look off into the distance with his nose in the air; he looks candidly at the viewer, modest and genuine, as though he is your Uncle George who pulls coins out of his ears and balances teapots

I'M THE EARL OF BRISTOL AND DON'T I LOOK SMASHING!

OH, BROTHER.

88. Gainsborough, Thomas (1727-1788). *Augustus John, Third Earl of Bristol.* 1768. Oil on canvas, 91.5 x 60 in. Ickworth National Trust, Suffolk, England.

89. Peale, Charles Willson (1741-1827). *George Washington at Princeton.* 1779. Oil on canvas, 93 x 58.5 in. Pennsylvania Academy of the Fine Arts, Philadelphia, Pennsylvania (Gift of Maria McKean Allen and Phebe Warren Downes through the bequest of their mother, Elizabeth Wharton McKean).

90. Peale, Charles Willson (1741-1827). *George Washington at Princeton*. 1779. Oil on canvas, 91.63 x 58.38 in. United States Senate, Washington D.C.

91. Peale, Charles Willson (1741-1827). *Washington After the Battle of Princeton, January 3, 1777.* 1779-1782. Oil on canvas, 96.5 x 61.5 in. Princeton University Art Museum, Princeton, New Jersey (bequest of Charles A. Munn, Class of 1881).

on his head at family get-togethers. Perhaps it is not an accident that Washington looks so familiar in Peale's portrait. Peale knew Washington; he fought beside him at the Battle of Princeton.

Finally, the time of day is significant. There is hint of a sunrise in the background. This reminds the viewer that the Battle of Princeton began at dawn, but it could mean more. Some critics suggest that perhaps Peale intended the dawn to represent the beginning of a new era, the dawning of a new country. The flag that rises at the back of the painting just above the horse's head mimics the rising of the sun in the early morning sky.

This portrait is going to be a big hit and Peale knows it. He has already begun painting copies for orders from as far away as France, Spain and Cuba (figures 90-91). So if you have a substantial amount of cash and don't mind George looming over your dining room table, you too can own a piece of this auspicious battle and hope with the rest of us that this image symbolizes the rise of something big.

LOOSE CANNON BALLS! PAGE 156!

Forgery

Compare this painting with the original on the left. Find ten differences. Answers are on page 192.

Original

Compare this painting with the forgery on the right. Find ten differences. Answers are on page 192.

15

The Art of Raphaelle Peale

AMERICAN ARTIST:
RAPHAELLE PEALE
Annapolis, MD

BORN
February 17, 1774

DIED
March 4, 1825

Forbidden Fruit

In which we learn why artists paint portraits and why canaries can't cook breakfast.

LEMONS AND PEACHES AND PEARS, OH MY!

PHILADELPHIA, SOMETIME IN 1823

Local artist Raphaelle Peale (figure 92) is quietly waging his own war against the status quo. How, you ask? Does he grow his hair long, wear bell-bottomed bloomers, keep screaming lemurs in his outhouse? Nope, he paints still life. Strange still life? Canvases loaded with deviant doohickies? Goofy gizmos? Whimsical whatchamacallits? Not at all. He paints normal, commonplace, everyday still life.

PORTRAITS ARE PARAMOUNT

But the question that makes him radical is not what does he paint, but what doesn't he paint? The answer is: portraits. For artists in this day and age, portraits are paramount. If you want to make money, if you want the respect of your peers and (perhaps most importantly) if you want to please your father you have to paint portraits. By choosing still life, Raphaelle has turned his back on the established painting world.

Stop any artist on the street and he will tell you that painting still life is for amateurs, apprentices, bush leaguers and greenhorns.

92. Peale, Charles Willson (1738-1815). *Raphaelle Peale.* 1817. Oil on canvas, 29 x 24 in. Private collection.

29

In the Peale household expectations are high; painting portraits a must.

Professional artists paint portraits. This is simply common knowledge. One cannot make a career out of copying grapes, lemons or the occasional fig. Where is the challenge in that? Peaches don't have personality. Apples have no character to capture. Oranges do not emote; they just sit. They are still. How difficult can that be?

And what about the money? Wealthy clients pay good money to have their likenesses captured on canvas. When was the last time a pear paid for his portrait? Fruit pays no fees. Cantaloupes don't commission paintings. Painting bacon doesn't, well, bring home the bacon. Relying on still life for a salary is a little like depending on your pet canary to cook breakfast.

Perhaps it is a question of capability. Can Raphaelle paint portraits? Is he talented? Well-trained? The answer is yes. He is not only proficient; he's brilliant. And despite his reputation, he has dabbled in the occasional portrait, though under some duress (figure 93). From where is that duress derived? Who is behind the scenes twisting his arm, so to speak? The man who trained him: his father.

PRESSURED BY HIS PADRE

Who is his father? He is none other than the famous portrait artist, scientist, paleontologist, and all-around talented guy, Charles Willson Peale. Though by most accounts a nice guy, Chuck does know how to put on the pressure. Not only did he name all of his children

after famous artists or scientists, but he also trained them from earliest

RAPHAELLE REALLY IS QUITE A GOOD PORTRAIT PAINTER. LOOK AT THE SENSITIVE EYES, THE SOFT FEATURES, THE INTELLIGENT GAZE . . . AND THE BOY LOOKS PRETTY GOOD TOO.

93. Peale, Raphaelle (1774-1825). *Portrait of Osborne Sprigg.* 1820. Oil on canvas, 30.25 x 24.5 in. Maryland Historical Society, Baltimore, Maryland.

childhood to draw and paint.

In the Peale household expectations are high. Success is important, painting portraits a must. So it appears that while Raphaelle paints cherries and grapes, he is also giving his old man the proverbial raspberry.

STILL LIFE WITH OSTRICH EGG CUP

Critics have pointed to one of Raphaelle's paintings in particular that pooh-poohs portraits most poetically: *Still Life with Strawberries and Ostrich Egg Cup* (figure 94). How does this piece of

A vanitas painting reminds the viewer of the emptiness or futility of life.

INSPIRING YOU TO PIC UP A BRUSH AND GET TO WORK? IT GETS BETTER.

art secretly sneer at authority? When artists draw a portrait, a head, a face, the basic shape is . . . yep, you guessed it, an ovoid or egg shape. It is as though Raphaelle has said, "You want a portrait? Here it is!" It's the Mr. Potato Head of the eighteenth century awaiting eyes, nose and a mouth that will never come.

WE'LL NEVER KNOW FOR SURE

Of course all of this is just speculation. Perhaps Raphaelle just likes painting food. We'll probably never know as he is quite tight-lipped, a bit of a recluse. And until he comes out with an autobiography entitled *Why I Paint*

Still Life and What Exactly They Mean, we can only guess.

Knowing us we will continue to pry until the cows come home, but until then we submit that Raphaelle is waging war, mounting hostilities, battling his own private demons, and that his exquisite paintings are a contentious comment on the state of the artistic world.

94. Peale, Raphaelle (1774-1825). ***Still Life with Strawberries and Ostrich Egg Cup.*** 1822. Oil on panel, 12.25 x 19.25 in. Private collection.

95. Peale, Raphaelle (1774-1825). ***Still Life with Cake.*** 1822. Oil on panel, 9.5 x 11.38 in. Private collection.

POPPY'S PROPS

BEST IN TOWN!

LIKE TO PAINT STILL LIFE?

TIRED OF PAINTING THE SAME OLD STUFF? IS YOUR WAX FRUIT MELTING IN THE SUN? DOES AUNT IRMA WANT HER SILVER CANDLESTICKS BACK? NEED SOME NEW SUBJECTS? COME ON DOWN TO POPPY'S PROPS AND BREATHE SOME NEW LIFE BACK INTO THAT STILL PAINTING. WE'VE GOT COATS, ROPES, CLOCKS, SOAPS, PANS, BEARS, MUFFINS, PEARS, BOATS, CARROTS, DONUTS, PARROTS, TEAPOTS, EGGS, VASES, KEGS, PLASTIC PIGS, VIKING HATS, RUBBER DUCKS AND BASEBALL BATS. YOU NAME IT; WE'VE GOT IT.

RUN, DON'T WALK TO POPPY'S TODAY!

Original

Compare this painting with the forgery below. Find ten differences. Answers are on page 193.

Forgery

Compare this painting with the original above. Find ten differences. Answers are on page 193.

PENNSYLVANIA PRATTLE

American Art History, Vol. No. 1   Bingo Card No. 30   artk12.com

AMERICAN ARTIST:
RAPHAELLE PEALE
Annapolis, MD

BORN
February 17, 1774

DIED
March 4, 1825

Still Life, Moving Death

In which we learn what vanitas are, and how bubbles, flowers, games and peeling fruit can be extremely depressing.

A PAINTING TO DIE FOR

PHILADELPHIA, SOMETIME IN 1823

Raphaelle's still life paintings may be a kind of rebellion, defiance or single-souled insurgency, but let's get more personal. In all honesty Raphaelle is not a specimen of robust health. He has logged too many hours in his father's science museum as a taxidermist and, regrettably, suffers from mercury and arsenic poisoning (two metals that are used in the preserving of animal corpses). On top of this it is rumored that he is depressed and spends too much time hitting the old bottle, so to speak.

VANITAS

With a crumbling constitution, plus a natural penchant for the poetic, Raphaelle probably thinks a lot about death. Death is not only a traditional ending to most lives, it is also the subject of a traditional type of still life painting called *vanitas*. The word *vanitas* means "emptiness" or vanity. A *vanitas* painting reminds the viewer of the emptiness or futility of life. Sound happy? Inspiring you to pick up a brush and get to work? It gets better.

Vanitas paintings usually include certain symbolic images that represent the short,

96. Peale, Raphaelle (1774-1825). ***Still Life with Peach.*** 1816. Oil on canvas, 7.36 x 8.42 in. San Diego Museum of Art, San Diego, California.

30

97. Cezanne, Paul (1839-1906). ***Still Life with Skull, Candle and Book.*** 1866. Oil. Private collection.

98. French School. ***Vanitas***. Louvre, Paris, France.

hollow, trifling side of life. Flowers, leaves and rotting fruit are all fragile and remind the viewer that things decay quickly; beauty only lasts a short while before ugliness and old age set in. Books, games, musical instruments and peeling fruit also represent things that come to an end. Skulls, of course, are also an obvious symbol of death, and candles have long represented the brevity of life. More common reminders are hourglasses, bubbles, mirrors and smoke (figures 97-98).

Granted, Raphaelle does not employ all of these symbols in his works, neither do all critics agree that his pieces are *vanitas*, but we think it might be worth looking into.

PAINTING PRODUCE

Though he does not use all, Raphaelle certainly uses many of the traditional *vanitas* symbols in his paintings, especially leaves, flowers, and fruit. Most of his still life canvases contain these in one form or another. In fact he

paints so much produce that one might suspect that he is channeling Old MacDonald or Johnny Appleseed, but I digress.

STILL LIFE WITH PEACH

It is important to notice that the pieces of fruit in Raphaelle's paintings are not perfect; they're flawed, pitted, bruised, scratched and in some cases just plain rotting. In his beautiful canvas, *Still Life with Peach* (figure 96) Raphaelle paints an exquisite peach, perfectly ripened with a rosy blush, delicately attached to a stem and adorned with fresh leaves. Yet when you look closer, there is a large dent in the fruit, a blemish, a bruise. In another of his pieces, *Still Life with Celery and Wine* (figure 99), the celery is wilted and the apples are practically rotting.

Remember, these are not photographs; they don't have to show imperfections. He could

CREEPY SKULL ON PAGE 166!

HEE HEE!

99. Peale, Raphaelle (1774-1825). ***Still Life with Celery and Wine.*** 1816. Oil on canvas, 12.38 x 17.13 in. Munson-Williams-Proctor Arts Institute, Utica, New York.

100. Peale, Raphaelle (1774-1825). ***Still Life with Steak.*** c. 1817. Oil on canvas, 13.38 x 19.5 in. Munson-Williams-Proctor Arts Institute, Utica, New York.

have painted the fruit unblemished, undamaged, whole. So unless Mr. Peale is campaigning for vegetable rights and these are his poster children, it would behoove us to admit that he is trying to tell us about something more important than apples and peaches.

MORE IMPORTANT THAN PEACHES?

What's could possibly be more important than apples and peaches you ask? What is Raphaelle's message? Fruit rots? Melon's mold? Applesauce happens? On one level, the most obvious or literal level, that is the message. Things die. But on another level Raphaelle is saying that just as fruit rots and dies, we will also die. Existence is short. Flesh is fleeting. Life is like a chicken coop ladder: dinky and dungy.

STILL LIFE WITH STEAK

But Raphaelle doesn't just paint fruit, he also paints meat. Not dainty displays of pan-seared chicken cordon bleu resting comfortably on a bed of steamed asparagus or filet mignon grilled to perfection still sizzling on the platter, but cold cuts of raw meat slapped on the table, no condiments, no plate. What's up with that?

In *Still Life with Steak* (figure 100) he paints a slab of raw beef accompanied by a head of cabbage and two carrots. Again, it is strangely reminiscent of a portrait: green leafy head, carrot appendages and a torso of meat. It's a personification: meat and vegetables as human body. It is flesh, dead flesh that will soon rot and smell. It almost makes you want to take the canvas out and bury it. But that's the point. It's death again, but this time, it's mammalian. Meat has muscle and fat, blood and bone, just like us. "This is you," says Raphaelle, "in 40 years, or 20 or 10 or 5."

DEPRESSED YET?

Depressing stuff from a depressed man? Maybe. But *vanitas* paintings aren't made for despair, they're created to move you, to motivate you to use wisely the time you have left. They're as much about life as they are death. Although the fruit threatens to rot and the meat threatens to stink, it never will. It will always remain on the brink; always there to remind you.

"Yes," Raphaelle might say, "Life is raw and tough, and death looms over all, but the purpose of these paintings is not to depress you but to enliven you, to remind you that there is still life to be lived, to encourage you to pick that fruit, smell those flowers. Not living is more tragic than dying; frittering away the hours on frivolities, a fate worse than death."

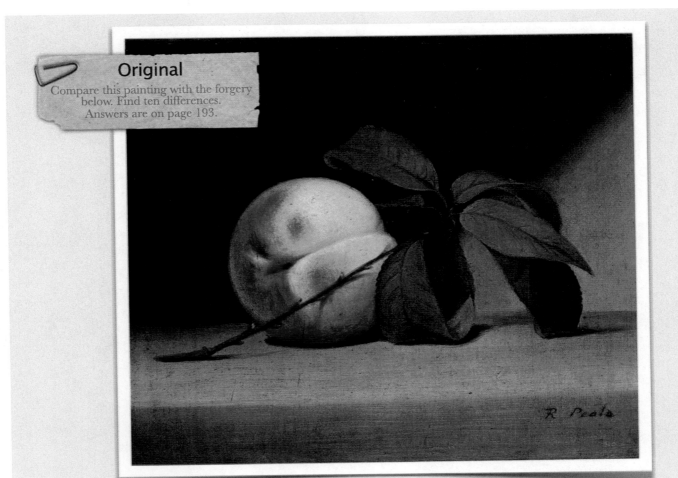

Original

Compare this painting with the forgery
below. Find ten differences.
Answers are on page 193.

Forgery

Compare this painting with the original
above. Find ten differences.
Answers are on page 193.

16
The Art of Gilbert Stuart

AMERICAN ARTIST:
GILBERT CHARLES STUART
Saunderstown, RI

BORN
December 3, 1755

DIED
July 9, 1828

A Plethora of Portraits

In which we learn more than we'd like to know about the Jay Treaty and that George Washington's body was shaped like a pear.

PAINTING PORTRAITS OF THE PRESIDENT

WHITE HOUSE, WASHINGTON D.C., 2004

On the 190th anniversary of the burning of Washington D.C. by British forces during the war of 1812, we here at the *Philadelphia Flurry* are interviewing Mr. Doughntuch Ennithang, curator of art and antiquities at the White House in Washington D.C.

US: Welcome to the *Flurry.* Thank you for taking time out of your busy schedule to join us and talk about the *George Washington (The Lansdowne Portrait)* (figure 101).

ENNITHANG: My pleasure.

US: The first question our readership may want answered is: what does the anniversary of the British attack on Washington D.C. have to do with *The Lansdowne Portrait?*

ENNITHANG: Excellent question. The answer is: nothing.

US: Nothing?

ENNITHANG: Yes. Nothing.

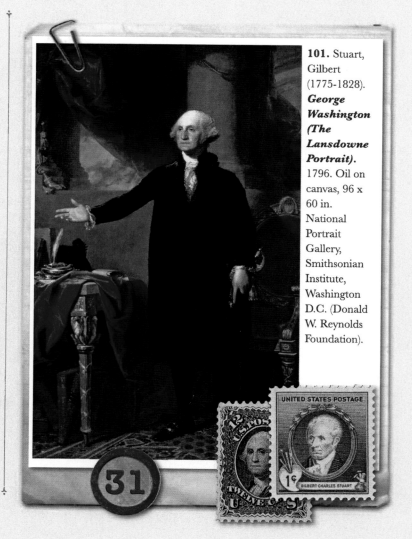

101. Stuart, Gilbert (1775-1828). *George Washington (The Lansdowne Portrait).* 1796. Oil on canvas, 96 x 60 in. National Portrait Gallery, Smithsonian Institute, Washington D.C. (Donald W. Reynolds Foundation).

102. Munger, George (1775-1828). *The President's House.* c. 1814-1815. Watercolor on paper, 11.9 x 15.7 in. White House Historical Association, White House, Washington D.C.

I'M THE WHITE HOUSE AFTER THE BRITISH BURNED ME IN 1814. WHAT A MESS!

US: I thought that Dolley Madison heroically rescued this painting from the White House just before the British set it on fire during the War of 1812?

ENNITHANG: She did.

US: Explain, please.

ENNITHANG: Certainly. Dolley Madison did save this portrait during the war of 1812 (or rather she made sure someone saved it) but this is not *The Lansdowne Portrait.* This is a copy of *The Lansdowne Portrait.*

US: A copy?

ENNITHANG: Gilbert Stuart painted the original *George Washington (The Lansdowne Portrait)* from life; then he later made a few copies of this portrait in his studio before he sent the original to England. The portrait you see here in the White House is one of those copies.

US: I see. How did the original wind up in England?

ENNITHANG: A man named William Bingham commissioned the original

Lansdowne Portrait as a gift for the Marquis of Lansdowne, a member of the British Parliament who sympathized with the colonists in their quest for independence.

US: Interesting. It looks huge. How big is it?

ENNITHANG: It is life-sized. In other words George stands over six feet tall on the eight-foot by five-foot canvas.

US: Wow.

ENNITHANG: I agree.

US: He looks different in this portrait compared to the portrait Charles Willson Peale made of him (see figure 86 on page 153). Here he looks very solid and well-proportioned. In Peale's portrait he looks all gangly and well, pear-shaped.

ENNITHANG: Washington does look considerably different in the two canvases.

US: Why?

"I insist on waiting until the large picture of Gen. Washington is secured, and it requires to be unscrewed from the wall. This process was found too tedious for these perilous moments; I have ordered the frame to be broken, and the canvass taken out."

- Dolley Madison in a letter to her sister.

George stands over six feet tall on the eight-foot by five-foot canvas.

THE PAINTING IS LIFE-SIZED.

ENNITHANG: Peale's portrait is more realistic. Even Washington's step-grandson admitted that. He also criticized Stuart's portrait as "failing entirely" to represent the General's frame.

The reason is simple. Stuart did not expect Washington to stand while he painted the entire portrait, he just rendered his head from life. For the body he used a stand-in.

US: A body double to do all of the difficult stunts?

ENNITHANG: I suppose you could put it that way.

US: Let's get down to the nitty-gritty and discuss the meat of the painting.

ENNITHANG: Okay, what do you want to know?

US: Symbolism, we love symbolism.

ENNITHANG: Well, there is plenty of it in this painting.

US: I suspected there was. Lay it on us, man.

ENNITHANG: Let's begin with Washington's suit.

US: Yeah, what's with the posh, black velvet and lace? Peale painted him in his military uniform.

ENNITHANG: Exactly. That was George the military general. This is George the civilian president.

US: But what about the sword?

ENNITHANG: This is a dress sword, not a military sword. Though it may have seen some action in the past, here it is clearly ceremonial,

not functional. It represents the democratic role the President plays in the United States. He is not a monarch who rules by the sword; he is a representative of the people.

US: So old George is just accessorizing?

ENNITHANG: Right.

US: I also see the old Stars and Stripes on the chair behind Washington (figure 105).

ENNITHANG: That is the shield from the Great Seal of the United States. The thirteen stars and thirteen stripes represent the first thirteen states in the union. The gold laurel around the shield symbolizes the victory in the War for Independence. You can also see

103. Peale, Charles Willson (1741-1827). ***George Washington at Princeton.*** 1779. Oil on canvas, 93 x 58.5 in. Pennsylvania Academy of the Fine Arts, Philadelphia, Pennsylvania (Gift of Maria McKean Allen and Phebe Warren Downes through the bequest of their mother, Elizabeth Wharton McKean).

104. Stuart, Gilbert (1775-1828). ***George Washington (The Lansdowne Portrait).*** 1796. Oil on canvas, 96 x 60 in. National Portrait Gallery, Smithsonian Institute, Washington D.C. (Donald W. Reynolds

WOW! THIS GEORGE REALLY DOES LOOK MORE LANKY AND GANGLY.

I'M GEORGE THE CIVILIAN AND THIS IS MY ALTER EGO, GEORGE THE MILITARY MAN.

BE NICE.

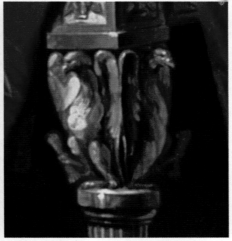

105-106. Stuart, Gilbert (1775-1828). *George Washington (The Lansdowne Portrait)* (details). 1796. Oil on canvas, 96 x 60 in. National Portrait Gallery, Smithsonian Institute, Washington D.C (Donald W. Reynolds Foundation).

the eagle from the Seal carved into the top of the table leg (figure 106).

US: I love this stuff. Is there more?

ENNITHANG: Are you kidding? Look at the books under the table (figure 107). If you get up close to the painting you can read the titles: *General Orders, American Revolution,* and *Constitution & Laws of the United States.* These volumes represent Washington's past and the Country's past. Washington was a general in the American Revolution and helped form the Constitution and laws of the United States, events that took place before the colonies became a country and before Washington became their president.

US: Fascinating. So what do the books on the table represent (figure 108)? His current bed time reading?

ENNITHANG: Not exactly. Their titles are: *Federalist* and *Journal of Congress.* They represent the present, the things

that the newly formed government was working on.

US: What about the blank paper (figure 108)?

ENNITHANG: Experts debate about the blank paper. Perhaps it represents history yet unwritten, the future, and the fact that George and Congress will have a big part in that.

US: Where does Congress come in? No congressmen are in the painting.

ENNITHANG: I forgot to mention something. In the painting Washington stands in the Hall of Assembly addressing Congress.

US: That makes more sense. What is he talking about?

ENNITHANG: As usual, critics do not agree. Some say he is giving his farewell address to Congress at the end of his second term.

US: Sounds logical.

I'M THE EAGLE ON THE DYE OF THE FIRST SEAL OF THE UNTED STATES. I WAS MADE IN 1782. THEY STOPPED PRESSING MY FACE INTO IMPORTANT PIECES OF PAPER IN 1841. THE NEW DYE LOOKS PRETTY MUCH THE SAME.

The books under the table represent Washington's past and the country's past.

THE BLANK PAPER REPRESENTS THE FUTURE, HISTORY YET UNWRITTEN.

ENNITHANG: Perhaps, except that Washington never gave a farewell address. He wrote it out and published as a public letter.

US: Oh. That throws a wrench into the monkey's theory.

ENNITHANG: You mean it throws a monkey wrench into the theory?

US: Um, yeah.

ENNITHANG: It does. Other critics claim that it represents Washington's address to Congress in December of 1795, in which he supported the "Jay Treaty."

US: Now I'm lost. What does the "Jay Treaty" have to do with anything?

ENNITHANG: It's complicated, but I will try to simplify. Bingham, the wealthy Philadelphian man who commissioned the painting, gave it to the Marquee of Lansdowne, a wealthy British man. These two men together with John Jay, the man the treaty is named after, all knew each other, all had had their portraits painted by Stuart and all were in favor of the "Jay Treaty," which promised open trade between the United States and Great Britain. How's that?

US: Concise yet confusing.

ENNITHANG: Let me sum up. The "Jay Treaty" passed with Washington's help and Bingham celebrated by commissioning Stuart to paint a portrait of Washington for the Marquis of Lansdowne.

US: Got it. Whew! You know, it reminds me of the Iroquois celebrating or sealing treaties by exchanging wampum belts.

ENNITHANG: That's an interesting connection. In 1783, when the British and the Americans signed the Treaty of Paris, Benjamin West painted a portrait of the signers. There are other examples of portraits being exchanged over treaties. In fact today when treaties are made we still take photographs of the signers.

107-108. Stuart, Gilbert (1775-1828). *George Washington (The Lansdowne Portrait)* (details). 1796. Oil on canvas, 96 x 60 in. National Portrait Gallery, Smithsonian Institute, Washington D.C (Donald W. Reynolds Foundation).

109-110. Stuart, Gilbert (1775-1828). *George Washington (The Lansdowne Portrait)* (details). 1796. Oil on canvas, 96 x 60 in. National Portrait Gallery, Smithsonian Institute, Washington D.C (Donald W. Reynolds Foundation).

US: Wow, I'm not sure my brain can hold any more. Are we almost finished?

ENNITHANG: There's only one more symbol I want to mention.

US: Go ahead. I'll concentrate.

ENNITHANG: Thanks. Look at the sky in the background. What do you see?

US: On the left I see storm clouds (figure 109) and on the right I see a rainbow (figure 110).

ENNITHANG: Any ideas?

US: Rain in the forecast, with baskets of gold? Perhaps George should have brought an umbrella; velvet doesn't hold up well in the rain.

ENNITHANG: Hmmm. Let me try. The storm clouds represent the war and all of the trouble and suffering that it caused. The rainbow on the right symbolizes peace and hopefulness, in other words the good weather, that the union of the states would bring.

US: By the way, is the original *Lansdowne Portrait* still in England?

ENNITHANG: Nope. In 1968 an anonymous person loaned the painting to the Smithsonian's National Portrait Gallery. In 2001 the Donald W. Reynolds Foundation bought it and gave it a permanent home in the National Portrait Gallery as a gift to the nation.

US: How much did that cost?

ENNITHANG: Thirty million dollars.

US: Wow! So it began here as a gift and ended up here as a gift.

ENNITHANG: Exactly.

US: Thanks for your time. You're really good at explaining things.

ENNITHANG: Thanks, it's a gift.

Forgery

Compare this painting with the original on the left. Find ten differences. Answers are on page 193.

Original

Compare this painting with the forgery on the right. Find ten differences. Answers are on page 193.

PHILADELPHIA FLURRY

AMERICAN ARTIST:
GILBERT CHARLES STUART
Saunderstown, RI

BORN
December 3, 1755

DIED
July 9, 1828

American Art History, Vol. No. 1   Bingo Card No. 32   artk12.com

A Portrait Held Hostage

In which we learn some less-than-complimentary things about Gilbert Stuart and that George hated having his portrait painted.

STUART HIJACKS A PAINTING TO AUGMENT HIS INCOME

ARLINGTON, VIRGINIA, IN 1845

Today, we here at the *Philadelphia Flurry* are interviewing Mr. George Washington Parke Custis, step-grandson to George Washington, first president of the United States of America.

US: Good morning, Mr. Custis.

CUSTIS: Good morning.

US: So, you are George Washington's step-grandson? How well did you know him?

CUSTIS: Quite well. When I was about 8 years old my father died and George and Martha Washington brought my sister, Nelly, and I to live with them in the presidential house which was in New York city at the time (figure 112).

US: Did they adopt you?

CUSTIS: Informally, yes. We became their unofficial children. They were very kind and generous to Nellie and I.

111. Stuart, Gilbert (1775-1828). *George Washington (The Athenaeum Portrait).* 1796. Oil on canvas, 39.8 × 34.6 in. Jointly owned by the National Portrait Gallery, Smithsonian Institute, Washington, and the Museum of Fine Arts, Boston, (William Francis Warden Fund, John H. and Ernestine A. Payne Fund, Commonwealth Cultural Preservation

112. Savage, Edward (1761-1817). ***The Washington Family.*** 1789-96. Oil on canvas, 84 1/8 x 111 7/8 in. National Portrait Gallery, Washington D.C.

US: Excellent. We'd like to ask you some questions about the portraits that Gilbert Stuart painted of your step-grandfather-informally-adoptive-father.

CUSTIS: You can call him George.

US: Okay, let's begin with the *Athenaeum Portrait*. For starters, why is it called *George Washington (The Athenaeum Portrait)* (figure 111)? Why not just the *Portrait of George Washington*?

CUSTIS: That's a good question with a long answer.

US: We've got nothing but time.

CUSTIS: The short answer has two parts. One, there are so many portraits of Washington that simply calling it the *Portrait of George Washington* would be extremely confusing, so portraits of the General are named after places where they are housed or people who commissioned them.

Secondly, it's called *George Washington (The Athenaeum Portrait)* because it is owned by the Boston Athenaeum, one of the first libraries in United States.

US: That was pretty long, so I'm afraid to ask. What's the long answer?

CUSTIS: The long answer is that Gilbert Stuart was a swindler, a charlatan and a scoundrel.

US: Whoa. Calm down, sir. Those are strong words.

CUSTIS: He deserves stronger.

US: Start at the beginning. What happened?

CUSTIS: Well, the General did not like to sit for portraits, but he sat twice for Mr. Stuart, once for *The Vaughn Portrait* and once for *The Lansdowne Portrait*. Then he announced that he would never sit again.

THEY USED THE ATHENAEUM PORTRAIT TO DESIGN THE ONE DOLLAR BILL.

Gilbert Stuart was a swindler, a charlatan and a scoundrel.

WHOA. CALM DOWN, SIR. THOSE ARE STRONG WORDS.

US: Didn't his legs get tired?

CUSTIS: Ha, ha. I mean he would never sit for a portrait again.

US: Right. So why did he?

CUSTIS: Well, Mrs. Washington decided that she wanted a portrait of George for their home at Mount Vernon and convinced the President to subject himself just one more time for her.

US: Then what?

CUSTIS: The Washingtons made a deal with Stuart. He would paint a pair of portraits of Mr. and Mrs. Washington, keep them for a while to make copies, and then give them over to the Washingtons.

US: What do you mean he kept them to make copies?

CUSTIS: That's how most portrait artists make their "bread and butter" so to speak. They paint an original or life portrait, a portrait painted in front of a live subject, and then later in their studio they make copies of the portrait which they sell to other clients. You can just imagine how many patrons might want a portrait of the famous George Washington.

US: True. So Stuart did this with *The Athenaeum Portrait*?

CUSTIS: In spades. It is estimated that throughout his lifetime he made between 100-130 copies of it. His daughter, Jane, says that at the end of his life, Stuart could hand paint a copy in as little as two hours. He called them his "hundred dollar bills" because he sold each for one hundred dollars.

US: Fascinating.

CUSTIS: I suppose, except that he never returned the original to my grandmother.

US: The scoundrel!

CUSTIS: Indeed.

US: Why not?

CUSTIS: Because he made too much money selling copies to let it go. My grandmother repeatedly asked for it. She and the General even visited him in person to request it, but he refused.

After the General died, his personal secretary even wrote Stuart a letter kindly asking for the portrait, even still offering to pay, but Grandmother never saw the paintings again. When Gilbert Stuart died in 1828 the Boston Athenaeum acquired the paintings.

US: Paintings? Plural?

CUSTIS: Yes. Remember, they ordered a pair of portraits: one of my grandmother and one of the General.

US: Stuart kept both?

CUSTIS: Yep. He kept both and never finished either one.

US: Why did Stuart like *The Athenaeum Portrait* so much?

CUSTIS: Well, not only did Mr. Washington dislike sitting for portraits, but he was notoriously difficult to paint.

US: What exactly do you mean?

CUSTIS: Portraits are meant to convey more than simply what the subject looks like. They are supposed to communicate the person's character and personality as well.

When painting a portrait an artist has to have more than artistic skill. He has to be able to draw out the sitter's personality.

US: How do they do that?

CUSTIS: By making the sitter feel comfortable. Generally they do this by chatting with them about something they like. If they don't, the sitter will look stiff and uncomfortable. Gilbert Stuart prided himself in being able to evoke and capture a sitter's personality.

"What a business is this of a portrait painter! You bring him a potato and expect he will paint you a peach."

- Gilbert Stuart

113. Stuart, Gilbert (1775-1828). *Martha Washington (The Athenaeum Portrait).* 1796. Oil on canvas, 39.8 × 34.6 in. Jointly owned by the National Portrait Gallery, Smithsonian Institute, Washington, and the Museum of Fine Arts, Boston, (William Francis Warden Fund, John H. and Ernestine A. Payne Fund, Commonwealth Cultural Preservation Trust).

114. Stuart, Gilbert (1775-1828). *George Washington (The Athenaeum Portrait).* 1796. Oil on canvas, 39.8 × 34.6 in. Jointly owned by the National Portrait Gallery, Smithsonian Institute, Washington, and the Museum of Fine Arts, Boston, (William Francis Warden Fund, John H. and Ernestine A. Payne Fund, Commonwealth Cultural Preservation Trust).

US: But it didn't work with old George, huh?

CUSTIS: Nope. Stuart painted the General twice before and was not satisfied with the expression in the portrait either time.

US: Let me guess. In *The Athenaeum Portrait* he captured it?

CUSTIS: Bingo.

US: How? Did he hire clowns and musicians to entertain him and make him smile?

CUSTIS: Not exactly. Stuart tried talking about all of the things that he thought a great general and statesman would be interested in, like battles and history and politics.

US: It didn't work?

CUSTIS: Nope. Those topics left the General as cold as a North Atlantic Mackerel.

US: So what did he do?

CUSTIS: During his fruitless attempts at conversation Stuart happened to mention something about horses and old George just lit up like a Christmas tree on Christmas morning.

US: Horses?

CUSTIS: Yep. My grandfather was crazy about horses.

US: Amazing.

CUSTIS: Indeed, and the rest is history, as they say. Despite it's frustrating history, Gilbert's painting is the most famous portrait of Washington of all times. I just wish my grandmother could have enjoyed it.

"When I painted him, he had just had a set of false teeth inserted, which accounts for the constrained expression so noticeable about the mouth and lower part of the face."

-Gilbert Stuart speaking of George Washington

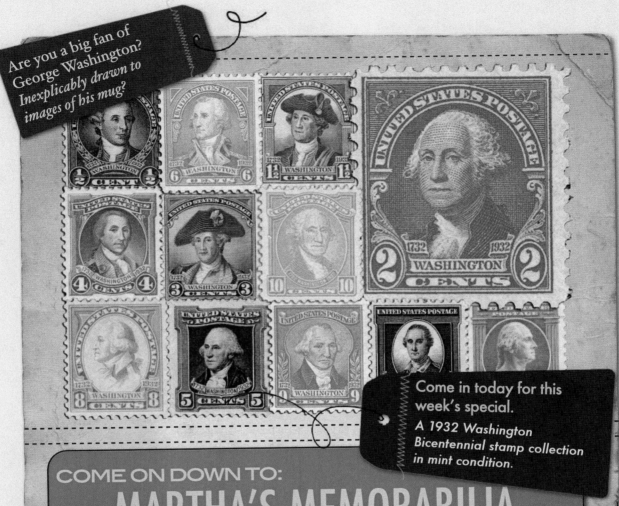

Are you a big fan of George Washington? Inexplicably drawn to images of his mug?

Come in today for this week's special.

A 1932 Washington Bicentennial stamp collection in mint condition.

COME ON DOWN TO:
MARTHA'S MEMORABILIA

Martha stocks her shelves full of all things Washington related.

She has mugs, jugs, cans, fans, dollars, collars, shirts, skirts, plates, crates, stamps, lamps, hats, mats, books, hooks, aprons, (Rats, nothing rhymes with aprons), posters, toasters, rocks, socks, oven mitts, bird house kits, bumper stickers, nose pickers, jelly jars, and candy bars. All with Washington's image on them. But this week's special is a full set of postage stamps issued in 1932 celebrating George Washington's 200th birthday. Each stamp is engraved with a different portrait painted by an early American artist. Included are four portraits painted by Charles Willson Peale, and two by Gilbert Stuart including his famous Athenaeum Portrait.

So if you are a Washington junkie, rush on down to Martha's Memorabilia and claim your crud today.

Forgery

Compare this painting with the original on the left. Find ten differences.
Answers are on page 193.

Original

Compare this painting with the forgery on the right. Find ten differences.
Answers are on page 193.

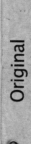

Recommended Readings

Below are some fiction and nonfiction children's books that can supplement the chapters in this volume. My student have thoroughly tested and enjoyed most of the titles listed. The reading levels vary and most of the books are still in print and available at most libraries. All are listed for purchase (new and used) on my website at: artk12.com/companion-books.

Chapter One: Prehistoric America

•Malam, John. *You Wouldn't Want to Be a Mammoth Hunter: Dangerous Beasts You'd Rather Not Encounter.*
•Harrison, David L. *Mammoth Bones and Broken Stones: The Mystery of North America's First People.* Boyds Mills Press, 2010.

Chapter Two: The Mound Builder Culture

•Searcy, Margaret. *Ikwa of the Mound-Builder Indians.* Firebird Press, 1989. An engaging story about a young Mound-Builder native, written by an anthropologist.
•Lorenz, Albert and Schleh, Joy. *Journey to Cahokia: A Boy's Visit to the Great Mound City.* Harry N. Abrams, 2004. A story about the pre-columbian city of Cahokia in Illinois, where the Birdman Tablet was found.
•Shemie, Bonnie. *Mounds of Earth and Shell.* Tundra Books, 1995.

Chapter Three: The Desert Southwest

•Crum, Sally. *Race to the Moonrise.* Western Reflections Publishing, Inc., 2006.

Chapter Four: The Iroquois Culture

•Taylor, C.J. *Peace Walker: The Legend of Hiawatha and Takanawita.* Tundra Books, 2004. An excellent retelling of the beginning of the Iroquois Confederacy.

•Fradin, Dennis Brindell. *Hiawatha: Messenger of Peace.* Margaret K. McElderry, 1992.

Chapter Five: The Taino Culture

•Danticat, Edwidge. *Anacaona: Golden Flower, Haiti, 1490.* Scholastic Inc., 2005. This is an excellent story about a Taino girl in Haiti on the eve of Columbus' arrival. An excellent view of Taino culture.
•Mann, Charles C. *Before Columbus: The Americas of 1491.* Atheneum Books for Young Readers, 2009. Excellent. Written by the author of *1491.*
•MacDonald, Fiona. *You Wouldn't Want to Sail with Christopher Columbus!: Uncharted Waters You'd Rather Not Cross.* Children's Press, 2004. One of the best history series available. Kids love it.

Chapter Six: The Art of John White

•Fritz, Jean. *The Lost Colony of Roanoke.* Putnam Juvenile, 2004.
•Stemple, Heidi E. Y. and Yolen, Jane. *Roanoke: The Lost Colony--An Unsolved Mystery from History.* Simon & Schuster, 2003.

Chapter Seven: The Art of Early Virginia

•Carbone, Elisa. *Blood on the River: James Town, 1607.* Puffin, 2007.
•Fritz, Jean. *The Double Life of Pocahontas.* Puffin, 2002.

Chapter Eight: Portraiture in Colonial America

Currently there are no children's books that directly address portraiture in Colonial America.

Chapter Nine: The Art of Matthew Pratt

Currently there are no books for children available on Matthew Pratt or early American portraiture.

Chapter Ten: Spanish Colonial Architecture

•Haley, Alex, Guzzi, George and Rawls, James J. *Never Turn Back: Father Serra's Mission.* Steck-Vaughn Company, 1993.
•Faber, Gail. *Pasquala: The Story of a California Indian Girl.* Magpie Publication, 1990.
•Jakes, John. *Susanna of the Alamo: A True Story.* Sandpiper, 1990.
•Rickman, David. *California Missions Coloring Book.* Dover Publications, 1992.

Chapter Eleven: The Art of Benjamin West

•Brenner, Barbara. *The Boy Who Loved to Draw: Benjamin West.* Sandpiper, 2003.
•Henry, Marguerite. *Benjamin West and His Cat Grimalkin.* Beautiful Feet Books, 2008.

Chapter Twelve: The Art of John Singleton Copley

•Flexner, James Thomas. *The Double Adventure of John Singleton Copley.* Little, Brown, 1969.

Chapter Thirteen: The art of Paul Revere

•Lawson, Robert. *Mr. Revere and I: Being an Account of Certain Episodes in the Career of Paul Revere, Esq. as Revealed by his Horse.* Little, Brown Books for Young Readers, 1998.
•Fritz, Jean. *And Then What Happened, Paul Revere?* Puffin, 1996.
•Rinaldi, Ann. *The Fifth of March: A Story of the Boston Massacre.* Graphia, 1993

Chapters Fourteen and Fifteen: The Art of Charles Willson Peale and Raphaelle Peale

•West, Tracey. *Mr. Peale's Bones.* Silver Moon, 2000.
•Tunnell, Michael O. *The Joke's on George.* Boyd Mills Press, 2001.
•Wilson, Janet. *The Ingenious Mr. Peale: Painter, Patriot, and Man of Science.* Athenaeum, 1996.

Chapter Sixteen: The Art of Gilbert Stuart

•Brown, Don. *Dolley Madison Saves George Washington.* Houghton Mifflin Books for Children, 2007. An easy picture book for all ages and a must for this chapter.
•Robinet, Harriette Gillem. *Washington City is Burning.* Athenaeum, 1996. An excellent retelling of the burning of Washington D.C. during the war of 1812. Written by a woman whose grandmother was a childhood slave on the Madison estate. Out of print, but worth tracking down.
•Chandra, Deborah. *George Washington's Teeth.* Square Fish, 2007.

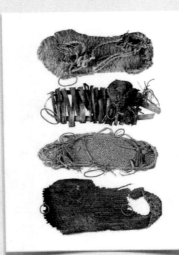

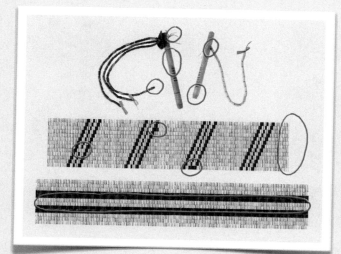

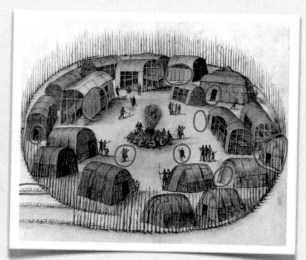

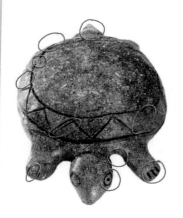

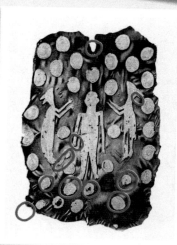

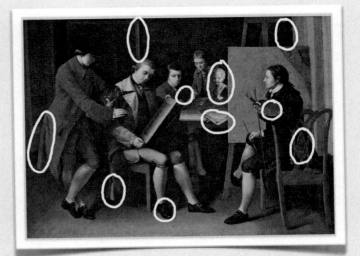

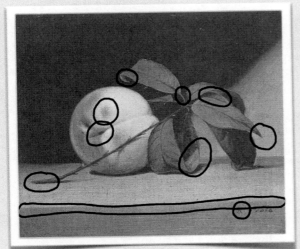

Picture Credits

Chapter 1
Clovis Spear Points: (spear points-top) Kristin Draeger ©2012, (spear points-bottom) Bill Whittaker CC-BY-SA-3.0/GNU license; (tools) Kristin Draeger ©2012
Prehistoric Tools: Kristin Draeger ©2012
Bingo numbers: iStockphoto.com/©2008 Christopher Conrad
All images unless otherwise noted: clipart.com
6: (stamp) iStockphoto.com/©2009 ray roper; **7**: (figure 2) wikimedia.org/PD, **10**: (stamp) iStockphoto.com/©2009 ray roper.

Chapter 2
Birdman Tablet: Kristin Draeger ©2012
Bannerstones: Kristin Draeger ©2012
Bingo numbers: iStockphoto.com/©2008 Christopher Conrad
All images unless otherwise noted: clipart.com
22: (stamp) iStockphoto.com/©2009 Lawrence Long.

Chapter 3
Mimbres Pottery: wikimedia.org/PD
Anasazi Sandals: National Parks Service/PD/Kristin Draeger ©2012.
Bingo numbers: iStockphoto.com/©2008 Christopher Conrad
All images unless otherwise noted: clipart.com
28: (figure 9) Kristin Draeger ©2012 after J. Walter Fewkes at ancestral.com, (stamp) iStockphoto.com/©2011 Sun Chan; **33**: (figure 11) Arkyan wikimedia.org/CC-BY-SA-3.0/GNU license.

Chapter 4
Hiawatha Wampum Belt: Kristin Draeger ©2012
Wampum Belts and Strings: Kristin Draeger ©2012.
Bingo numbers: iStockphoto.com/©2008 Christopher Conrad
All images unless otherwise noted: clipart.com
40: (NYstamp) iStockphoto.com/©2011 traveler1116, (stamp) wikimedia.org/USPS/PD; **41**: (beads) Kristin Draeger ©2012; **42**: (figure 18) wikimedia.org/NOAA Photo Library/PD, (figure 19) ChildofMidnight CC-BY-SA-3.0/GNU license; (figure 20) wikimedia.org/R. A. Nonenmacher/PD; **46**: (NYstamp) iStockphoto.com/©2011 traveler1116.

Chapter 5
Deminan Caracaracol: Kristin Draeger ©2012
Taino Turtle: Kristin Draeger ©2012

Bingo numbers: iStockphoto.com/©2008 Christopher Conrad
All images unless otherwise noted: clipart.com
52: (stamp) wikimedia.org/PD; **57**: (stamps) wikimedia.org/USPS/ PD; **59**: (illustration) Kristin Draeger ©2012.

Chapter 6
Indian Village of Pomeiock: clipart.com
Indians Fishing: clipart.com
Bingo numbers: iStockphoto.com/©2008 Christopher Conrad
All images unless otherwise noted: clipart.com
62: (stamp) iStockphoto.com/©2010 Jenny Speckels.

Chapter 7
Powhatan's Mantle: clipart.com
John Smith's Map of Virginia: Library of Congress/PD
Bingo numbers: iStockphoto.com/©2008 Christopher Conrad
All images unless otherwise noted: clipart.com
72: (stamps) wikimedia.org/USPS/ PD; **76**: (stamps) wikimedia.org/USPS/ PD;

Chapter 8
John Freake: wikimedia.org/PD
Elizabeth Clarke Freake (Mrs. John Freake) and Baby Mary: Dover ©2008
Self-Portrait of Captain Thomas Smith: Dover ©2008
Bingo numbers: iStockphoto.com/©2008 Christopher Conrad
All images unless otherwise noted: clipart.com
86: (stamps) wikimedia.org/USPS/PD; **87**: (figure 40) Dover ©2007; **88**: (figures 41-42) wikimedia.org/PD, (figure 43) Ricardo André Frantz CC-BY-SA-3.0 license.

Chapter 9
The American School: Dover ©2008
Bingo numbers: iStockphoto.com/©2008 Christopher Conrad
All images unless otherwise noted: clipart.com.

Chapter 10
Mission San Antonio de Valero: Daniel Schwen wikimedia.org/CC-BY-SA-3.0/GNU license
Mission San Diego de Alcalá: Dmadeo CC-BY-SA-3.0/GNU license
Bingo numbers: iStockphoto.com/©2008 Christopher Conrad
All images unless otherwise noted: clipart.com

104: (stamp) wikimedia.org/USPS/public domain;
106: (figure 55) Travis Witt 2010 wikimedia.org/CC-BY-SA-3.0/GNU license; **107**: (figure 65) E-roxo 2004 wikimedia.org/CC-BY-SA-3.0/GNU license; (figure 66) PMRMaeyaert 2009 wikimedia.org/CC-BY-SA-3.0 license; **110**: (mission stamp) Fotolia.com/rook76, (Father Serra stamp) Fotolia.com/Mark Markau.

Chapter 11

The Death of General Wolfe: Dover ©2008
William Penn's Treaty with the Indians: wikimedia.org/public domain
Bingo numbers: iStockphoto.com/©2008 Christopher Conrad
All images unless otherwise noted: clipart.com
116: (stamp) iStockphoto.com/©2012 Kenneth Wiedemann; **118**: (figure 62) wikimedia.org/public domain.

Chapter 12

Watson and the Shark: Dover ©2008
A Boy with a Flying Squirrel: Dover ©2008
Bingo numbers: iStockphoto.com/©2008 Christopher Conrad
All images unless otherwise noted: clipart.com
128: (stamp) iStockphoto.com/©2007 ray roper.

Chapter 13

Coffee Pot: wikimedia.org/Daderot/public domain
The Bloody Massacre: wikimedia.org/Library of Congress/public domain
Bingo numbers: iStockphoto.com/©2008 Christopher Conrad
All images unless otherwise noted: clipart.com
136: (stamps) wikimedia.org/USPS/public domain;
141: (stamp) wikimedia.org/USPS/public domain; (stamp printing press) Fotolia.com/AlexanderZam.

Chapter 14

Staircase Group: Dover ©2008
George Washington at Princeton: Dover ©2008
Bingo numbers: iStockphoto.com/©2008 Christopher Conrad
All images unless otherwise noted: clipart.com
146: (stamps) wikimedia.org/USPS/public domain;
147: (figure 82) wikimedia.org/Library of Congress's Geography & Map Division/public domain; **155**: (figure 88) wikipaintings.org/public domain; **156**: (figures 90-91) wikimedia.org/public domain.

Chapter 15

Still Life with Ostrich Egg Cup and Strawberries: the-athenaeum.org/public domain

Still Life with Peach: the-athenaeum.org/public domain
Bingo numbers: iStockphoto.com/©2008 Christopher Conrad
All images unless otherwise noted: clipart.com
160: (stamp) wikimedia.org/USPS/public domain;
161: (figure 92) wikimedia.org/public domain, (figure 93) the-athenaeum.org/public domain; **162**: (figures 95) the-athenaeum.org/public domain, ; **165**: (stamp) wikimedia.org/USPS/public domain; **166**: (figure 97) wikipaintings.org/public domain; **167**: (figure 99) the-athenaeum.org/public domain, (figure 100) the-athenaeum.org/public domain.

Chapter 16

George Washington (The Lansdowne Portrait): wikimedia.org/public domain
George Washington (The Athenaeum Portrait): wikimedia.org/public domain
Bingo numbers: iStockphoto.com/©2008 Christopher Conrad
All images unless otherwise noted: clipart.com
172: (stamps) wikimedia.org/USPS/public domain;
173: (figure 102) wikimedia.org/public domain; **174**: (figure 103) Dover ©2008; **175**: (figure 105) Dover ©2008, (Great Seal) wikimedia.org/public domain/ United States Dipomacy Center; **180**: (stamps) wikimedia.org/USPS/public domain; **181**: (figure 112) wikimedia.org/public domain; **184**: (figure 113) wikimedia.org/public domain.

Made in the USA
Columbia, SC
25 September 2020